Cognitive Structures
and Religious Research

Cognitive Structures

and Religious Research

ESSAYS IN SOCIOLOGY AND THEOLOGY

by

W. WIDICK SCHROEDER

East Lansing
MICHIGAN STATE UNIVERSITY PRESS
1970

★
  ★
 ★
  ★
  ★

MANUFACTURED IN THE UNITED STATES OF AMERICA

To Scott and Carla, whose generation will be the next to reflect upon the issues explored here.

Acknowledgments

Grateful acknowledgment is hereby made for permission to quote from the following copyrighted material:

The City, by Max Weber, reprinted with permission of The Macmillan Company. © The Free Press, a Corporation 1958; *The Divine Imperative*, by Emil Brunner, translated by Olive Wyon, reprinted with permission of The Westminster Press. Copyright 1947, by W. L. Jenkins; *The Eclipse of Community: An Interpretation of American Studies*, by Maurice R. Stein, reprinted with permission of Princeton University Press. Copyright 1960 by Princeton University Press; *The Elementary Forms of the Religious Life*, by Emile Durkheim, reprinted with permission of The Macmillan Company. Copyright 1915 by George Allen & Unwin, Ltd.; *From Max Weber: Essays in Sociology*, by Max Weber, translated and edited by H. H. Gerth and C. Wright Mills, reprinted with permission of Oxford University Press. Copyright 1946 by Oxford University Press; *The Nature and Destiny of Man*, by Reinhold Niebuhr, reprinted with permission of Charles Scribner's Sons. Copyright 1949 by Charles Scribner's Sons; *Process and Reality*, by Alfred North Whitehead, reprinted with permission of The Macmillan Company. Copyright 1929 by The Macmillan Company; *The Rules of Sociological Method*, by Emile Durkheim, reprinted with permission of The Macmillan Company. Copyright © 1938 by The University of Chicago; *The Social System*, by Talcott Parsons, reprinted with permission of The Macmillan Company. Copyright 1951 by Talcott Parsons; *Sociology and Philosophy*, by Emile Durkheim, reprinted with permission of The Macmillan Company. Copyright 1953 by The Free Press of Glencoe; *The Theory of Social and Economic Organization*, by Max Weber, translated by A. R. Henderson and Talcott Parsons, reprinted with permission of The Macmillan Company. Copyright 1947 by Talcott Parsons; "Urbanism as a Way of Life" by Louis Wirth, reprinted with permission of The University of Chicago Press. Copyright 1938 by The University of Chicago.

Preface

These essays are the result of my interest in actual and possible relations between sociology and theology. My interest in these relations was aroused while a graduate student in sociology at Michigan State University studying with the late Paul Honigsheim, who had been a student of Max Weber and Ernst Troeltsch at Heidelberg shortly after the turn of the century. Intrigued by the lucidity of Weber's social analysis, I was also uneasy about his distinction between statements of fact and of value. Although I had not yet considered critically the neo-Kantian philosophic tradition undergirding Weber's affirmation, I did appreciate his persistent and consistent refusal to explain values and value affirmations definitively on the basis of social phenomena. By contrast, the perspective of Emile Durkheim, which did explain value orientations by social norms, did not satisfy me. Because of their importance for value orientations, religious phenomena were very important for both of these theroists. The different ways in which they interpreted them puzzled me.

As I was also concerned with the development of empirical research in the sociology of religion, two closely related interests came to focus. The first interest centered about the adequacy of explanations of social phenomena and the relation of these explanations to alternative philosophical and theological perspectives. In the broadest sense, the question of truth is inherent in these issues, since the theorist must take a stand regarding the informing structure which guides his work and orders his empirical data. The second interest centered about the methodology of empirical sociological studies of religious phenomena. Having decided among alternative theoretical schemata, the analyst must still resolve or compromise the question of the best way to gather, analyze and present data on religious phenomena. The essays in this book represent variations on these two interests.

Although I cannot acknowledge adequately my indebtedness to all who have contributed in various ways to these essays, I want especially to express my appreciation to the following who have contributed directly to the interests reflected here: Professor Emeritus Samuel C. Kincheloe and Victor Obenhaus of the Chicago Theological Seminary; Richard P. McKeon, W. Alvin Pitcher and Gibson Winter of the University of Chicago; the late Paul Honigsheim, J. Allan Beegle and W.

Lloyd Warner of Michigan State University; Bernard M. Loomer of Berkeley Baptist Divinity School and the Graduate Theological Union; James Luther Adams of Harvard University; and Charles Hartshorne of the University of Texas.

I want to thank the editors of the *Journal for the Scientific Study of Religion* and the *Review of Religious Research* for permitting me to include material based on articles which originally appeared in their journals.

I should also like to thank Mrs. Katherine Powers and Mrs. Carole Harmon who typed portions of various drafts of the manuscript. I am especially indebted to Mrs. Frances Ritsch and Mrs. Arlene Schneider, who shared responsibility for most of the typing, and to Mrs. Lark Cowling, who edited this book with perspicacity.

Finally, I should like to thank the students, faculty, and administrative officers of the Chicago Theological Seminary and the Divinity School of the University of Chicago and participants in the Center for the Scientific Study of Religion for providing the environment which stimulated many of the ideas developed in this work.

W. W. S.

Table of Contents

Introduction

These interrelated essays in theology and sociology are the result of work in a fairly new interdisciplinary area. Moreover, the issues under discussion are shaped and resolved through a mode of thought known as process philosophy. Alfred North Whitehead and Charles Hartshorne are among the most distinguished proponents of process philosophy, which is rooted in the Platonic tradition but involves inversions of Plato's general point of view.

Although they have attracted some attention in philosophical circles, process philosophy and dipolar theism, an integral part of this philosophic viewpoint, are relatively unfamiliar to most theologians and sociologists. Some theologians have been influenced by this general point of view, but its influence is still largely confined to a small group of American theologians. Because of the anti-metaphysical biases of most social scientists and the specialized nature of graduate education, the Whiteheadian perspective is even less common among contemporary social scientists.

Several reactions to the themes developed here may be anticipated. Many theologians may hold that these essays are too sociological and naturalistic; many social scientists, that they are too theological and formalistic. Nevertheless, the Whiteheadian perspective holds great promise for both the social sciences and theology: it can free the social sciences from a truncated mechanistic scientism and can offer theology a contemporary theistic naturalism which coheres with scientific understanding.

Two interests recur in this volume. The first centers on the exploration of alternative perspectives on the nature of social phenomena. These explorations are provisional and heuristic rather than final and normative, but they do involve normative issues. Fundamental human experiences—the experience of meaning, the contribution of past experience to that meaning, and the lure toward harmony and intensity of feeling—point to the inextricable interrelatedness of fact and value. This intermingling of fact and value means that it is not only permissible to raise questions of truth and value at any point in an analysis but also necessary to raise them at some points.

The second interest centers on appropriate modes for empirical studies of religious phenomena. The intertwining of fact and value means that these two interests are not sharply separable. Methodological perspectives have substantive implications, and vice versa, but these difficulties may be minimized in some empirical studies.

Although the reader may be put off by the frequent typological devices, these typologies are used to illumine alternative perspectives from which one might interpret social phenomena. One's understanding of his own viewpoint is enriched when that perspective is contrasted with alternatives; these explorations are not merely surveys of existing or possible viewpoints in theology or the social sciences but are intended to help the reader grasp and contrast his own viewpoint more clearly with alternatives.

Typologies must be grounded in some philosophical viewpoint, for there are no Olympian heights from which an unconditioned thinker may survey the world.[1] The typologies used here to characterize perspectives on the nature of reality and on methods of sociological analysis are based upon the formal components and dynamic processes fundamental in human experience: form, power, and a lure toward harmony and intensity of feeling through the unification of formal and dynamic dimensions of experience. In this unification, man is aware of both appropriating and transcending the past. The fourfold typologies of fundamental perspectives on reality and methods of sociological analysis developed in Parts One and Two are based on these components and processes.

A none-some-all triad guides the typological formulations which explore possible relations between entities or components of experience. This triad, in turn, is based on the most general geometric relations conceivable between two entities: independence, contiguity, overlap, and identity. This triad and the typology noted in the preceeding paragraph are both used in Part Four.

Because the typologies are based upon distinctions between the parts of a whole, those who maintain that a whole is more than the sum of its parts will believe that the typologies distort reality. The criticism is a legitimate one; however, the typologies have considerable heuristic value if they are employed with caution and restraint.

The fundamental human experience of the lure toward harmony and intensity of feeling is evidence of the inextricable intertwining of fact and value. Feeling precedes cognition, but both are necessary components of experience. One may begin his reflection with any subject matter, but he must consider questions of value if he presses his reflection adequately.[2] Therefore, such questions are raised in most of the following essays, although some chapters explore problems of evaluation more fully than others.

These essays are not completely autonomous. There are frequent allusions or references to ideas developed in one chapter in other contexts. Moreover, the same typological devices and evaluative framework are consistently employed. In spite of this unity, the topics are arbitrary in the sense that there is no unequivocally necessary reason for including these topics rather than other ones.

This book is divided into four parts. The balance between analytic and constructive dimensions in each chapter is conditioned by the subject matter and emphasis of that chapter. The constructive or critical dimension is most muted in Chapters I, III, and IV.

PART ONE, *Perspectives on the Social Sciences*, is composed of typological studies of various perspectives on sociology which examine the implications of these perspectives for sociological research. Chapter I, "Cognitive Structures and Religious Research," considers alternative perspectives on the ordering of the sciences and examines the consequences of these alternative viewpoints for research in the sociology of religion. The second chapter explores alternative views of social stratification and presents an interpretation of the implications of this phenomenon for Protestant churches in the United States. Various sociological approaches to the study of urban life are considered in Chapter III, but the methods discussed are also used to study other social phenomena, including religious ones.

PART TWO, *Empirical Applications*, illustrates methodological approaches to the sociology of religion. Chapter IV, "Lay Expectations of the Ministerial Role," presents research data at a moderate level of abstraction. The findings, based on interview data gathered by survey research techniques, are ordered by categories derived from theoretical considerations. The categories themselves are relatively neutral, so analysts informed by various perspectives may alter their substance somewhat. The effects of a normative schema have been minimized, though the notes offer some suggestions about such a schema.

Chapter V, "Protestant Involvement in Community Organizations with Special Reference to The Woodlawn Organization," illustrates a different type of research analysis. An examination of alternative perspectives on the nature of reality provides the basis for a typology of voluntary associations. A normative conceptual schema is used to order data gathered by observation, by informal discussions with participants in the organization, by informal discussions with critics of the organization, and by a study of various news releases. Normative understandings and empirical observations are discussed conjointly and judgments about the proper relation of Protestant churches to the organization are presented. Some social scientists will criticize this chapter as a hopeless intertwining of fact and value statements. However, an investigator who refuses to make evaluative judgments in some contexts may be guilty of irresponsibility and evasiveness. The most one may ask of an analyst is that he exercise self-conscious clarity about the approach he is using.

PART THREE, *Three Philosophical Sociologists*, containing both analytic and constructive material, permits a more specific and intensive examination of issues considered typologically in Part One. The ordering of the sciences developed by Max Weber, Emile Durkheim, and Talcott Parsons, three of the most influential sociological theorists of the twentieth century, are examined in an attempt to illumine the basic notions guiding their analyses.

Each of the chapters in this part follows a common pattern: the first three sections of the chapter undertake an internal analysis of the theorist's position; the final section presents an external critique of the theorist. This approach is fairly uncommon among contemporary social scientists in the United States, so some preliminary observations may be useful. The focus is exclusively upon the theorist's categorical ideas. These fundamental notions do not change and provide the framework for all other aspects of the sociologist's thought. The analyses are confined to selected crucial texts which present the theorists' basic notions; secondary sources are cited infrequently. The loss of breadth such a limitation imposes is more than offset by the depth considerations which such a treatment permits.

PART FOUR, *Theological Interpretations, Typological and Constructive*, deals primarily with theological interpretations of social phenomena, but relates them to sociological interpretations. The typologies developed in this part illumine the internal meaning of alternative theological viewpoints, all of which affirm the authenticity of a Subject-

Object of religious devotion Who is, in some sense, *sui generis.*

A social scientist who wants to understand a religious institution, a religious idea, or a devotee of a religious tradition must empathize with the institution, belief, or person. In order to do so, he must at least provisionally grasp the framework which informs the proponents of the religious tradition he is studying. It is far easier to enunciate this principle than it is to follow it, for the investigator himself must be guided by some framework. If the framework he affirms is too alien to the religious tradition whose protagonists he is studying, he may be unable to empathize with them. One of the objectives of Part Four is the development of a framework which illumines alternative interpretations of religious phenomena. Such a framework may help the analyst to understand the lure to the follower of a particular religious tradition, even though the participant himself responds vaguely to questions about his religious beliefs and experiences.

Chapter X, "Some Methodological Reflections on the Social Scientific Investigation of Sermonic Discourse and Religious Experience," considers both the question of different views on the nature of sermonic discourse and the problem of the vagueness of language and its relation to fundamental religious experience. The former question highlights the role which the research worker's framework plays in the selection of the subject matter for investigation; the latter question accentuates the problem which the ambiguity between words, feelings and authentic religious experience presents to those who use interviews and questionnaires in the investigation of religious experience.

The final two chapters are addressed primarily to religious professionals unhappy with fashionable interpretations of religion in American culture that disparage unduly local religious institutions, criticize inordinately existing forms of social organization in the United States, or sanctify too readily particular social, political, or economic programs and to social scientists uneasy about fashionable social scientific frameworks that explain religious phenomena on non-*sui generis* grounds, seek inordinate exactitude in social scientific investigations, and undercut efforts to use reason to guide evaluative judgments about the forms of social organization which can most adequately enhance men's lives together.

Chapter XI, "The Nature of Religious Institutions and the Role of the Religious Professional: Analytic and Constructive Perspectives," explores alternative God-world relations and the implications of these alternatives for one's understanding of the nature of the religious institution and the role of the religious professional. It is maintained that an interpreter's view of the relation between religion and culture is guided by his view of God-world relations. A discussion of the implications of alternative views is followed by a constructive interpretation.

Chapter XII, "Love, Justice and Forms of Social Organization," a continuation of the discussion begun in Chapter XI, develops a typology of possible love-justice relations and illustrates them with examples drawn from the Christian tradition. The final section presents a constructive view of the relation between love, justice and forms of social organization.

Every social scientist who studies religious phenomena and every religious professional who serves religious institutions must make a judgment about his own view of the nature of religion, the nature of the religious institution, the relation between religion and culture, the character of love and justice, and the implications of love-justice relations for forms of social organization. His view may be broader or narrower, depending on the range of possibilities he has pondered before he comes to his own judgment. In any event, he will move in one of the directions delineated in Chapter XI; if he affirms a *sui generis* option, he will move in one of the directions described in Chapter XII.

Each individual, informed by the desire for wholeness and integrity which the lure for truth evokes, must resolve these issues for himself. The Divine Reality which elicits religious experience will not be satisfied until men effect the supreme fusion between fact and value dimensions of experience. Social scientists informed by this vision may undertake a sympathetic and understanding *sui generis* interpretation of men's religious experience and of the beliefs and institutions which such experience has evoked. Religious professionals guided by such a vision may serve religious institutions with integrity. All men grasped by such a vision may attain greater internal harmony and may be guided and sustained in their quest for love and justice in the social order.

PART ONE

Perspectives on the Social Sciences:

Interpretations and Methods of Investigation

Chapter I

Cognitive Structures
and Religious Research[1]

The sociologist undertaking social scientific studies of religion will find his research efforts inextricably related to the type of cognitive structure informing his conception of the nature of sociology and its relation to the other sciences. His resolution of this issue will commit him, either explicitly or implicitly, to some philosophical or theological tradition.

The following section argues that the dominant cognitive structures in current American sociological discussions are informed primarily by the atomistic perspective of Democritus in classical Greek philosophy, by the skeptical view of the Greek Sophists, or by some combination of the two. The dominant cognitive structures in Christian theology are informed primarily by either Aristotelian or Platonic traditions. Most Catholic formulations are closely related to the Aristotelian tradition; most Protestant formulation, to some variant of the Platonic heritage. This chapter briefly treats epistemological and anthropological problems differentiating most Protestant theologians from Plato and the "natural-supernatural" distinction distinguishing many Roman Catholic theologians from Aristotle because these differences effect the ordering of the sciences.

Theoretical differences between most theologians and most sociologists are general because of the differences in their informing structures. They disagree about the nature of science and "religion," the meaning of power, freedom, history, love, and justice, method in the social studies, the nature and destiny of man, and the nature and character of God. Furthermore, the relationship between the researched "facts" and the cognitive structure employed by the analyst is at best obtuse.

Because the fashion of certain philosophic frameworks in sociology is a contingent and not a categorical matter, it may be useful to explore the issue of cognitive structures and religious research, especially the implications for religious research based on informing structures other than those currently fashionable in the social studies. A conversation between social scientists and theologians may prove productive. At present, however, it is difficult to initiate and conduct a significant discussion for the structure of university and theological education discourages it. Those who defend on principle a multiplicity of the sciences may be relatively satisfied with the present situation, but those who defend on principle some type of unity of the sciences may be relatively unhappy. Aristotle might have countenanced academic "departments," but Plato would have been disheartened if such institutional patterns became too rigid.

The role of popular sociological cognitive structures can be seen in other areas. For example, some current sociological theory makes it difficult to interpret data in the political order in terms other than those which suggest that political activity is unqualifiedly a power struggle. Floyd Hunter uses this approach in *Community Power Structure.*[2] Similarly, the classic formulations of Max Weber are informed by the understanding of power as the ability to achieve one's own will in conflict with other wills. On the other hand, Sir Ernst Barker stands in the Aristotelian tradition.[3] His *Reflections on Government* incorporates both normative and descriptive dimensions. The appropriate functions for various components of the political order are posited, so the analyst may then discern the extent to which these functions are being carried out by the appropriate organ.

On a somewhat more esoteric but suggestive and theoretically interesting level, current sociological cognitive structures make it difficult to order coherently psychic phenomena such as telepathy. Many in the Platonic tradition would be interested in such phenomena because their theoretic structure allows for its existence. Of course, the theoretic structure would not be dependent on the observational data of such phenomena, but positive findings would certainly support the theory.

The final section of this chapter considers the issue of research on substantive problems. It presupposes the fundamental difficulties about alternative cognitive structures discussed in the following section.

Alternative Relations Between Theology and Sociology

Considered formally, four broad approaches to the relation between theology and sociology are possible. Two of the formulations make distinctions between various disciplines; two argue for a basic unity of the sciences. One of the latter usually distinguishes between science and an area of non-science, including theology. Advocates of the unity of the sciences may focus either upon the coherence and universality of the components involved in experience, or upon the underlying fundamental elements which give rise to everything else. Those who argue for a multiplicity of the sciences may focus either upon the presence of different subject matters or upon the perspectives of different observers.

The manner in which an analyst arrives at an alleged multiplicity or unity of the sciences is very subtle. Because of epistemological and/or methodological differences, analysts may develop different bases for alleged unities or multiplicities and may posit different understandings of the nature of reality. Some may affirm provisional multiplicities related to an underlying unity. Some may entertain differences about the nature of the subject matter they are considering. Part Three considers these issues in more detail; in this chapter the relatively clear-cut characterizations apply explicitly to the figures or traditions cited.

Two classical traditions have tended to produce a multiplicity of the sciences. The first is embodied in the work of Aristotle who developed the classic distinctions between the theoretic, the practical, and the aesthetic disciplines. Each of these broad groupings contains additional generic and specific differentiations based upon subject matter; ultimately each discipline is set in its proper but distinct relationship to every other discipline. Clearly, this tradition allows work in the social sciences without necessarily involving the social scientist *qua* social scientist in ontological issues. Because of the clear-cut distinctions among the several disciplines, he may also legitimately focus on certain problems without entertaining explicit theological concerns. Historically, Roman Catholic sociologists most frequently sustain this perspective. Because of the concern of most sociologists with what in the Aristotelian tradition is called "efficient cause," there is some kinship between workers in this group and other sociologists; the latter group is almost invariably suspicious when Aristotelian or Thomist sociologists consider the necessity, from their point of view, of discussing other causes, particularly "final cause."

Diverse conceptions among protagonists about nature's end or purpose and the relation of the practical to the theoretic extenuate these differences. Because most contemporary sociologists are informed by alternative understandings of the nature of reality, they are inclined to be skeptical of the alleged existence of a supreme being, God, the subject matter of theology.

Because Aristotle locates freedom in the context of social and political institutions, all the social studies are placed in the "practical" disciplines. The social studies are concerned with actions initiated by the actor who may choose other actions than those which he has chosen. The vigorous Catholic opposition to Freud is also to be seen in relation to this Aristotelian understanding of human freedom. Contemporary proponents of this perspective, then, are apt to argue for a fundamental threefold organization of the sciences, as did Aristotle.[4]

A second group arguing for a multiplicity of the sciences is exemplified by the Sophists. Sophistic multiplicity, informed by a pervasive principle of relativity, is dependent upon the perspective of the observer. "Man is," said Protagoras, "the measure of all things."

Proponents of this perspective cannot appeal to objective criteria inherent in the nature of things. The differentiations made in the several disciplines are conventional and depend upon a consensus among workers in an area. Definitions in sociology, or any other area, are "operational." Freedom is defined in terms of one agent's ability to influence the overt or covert behavior of others; the free man is ultimately the strong man. Because they deny the presence of any transcendental dimensions, those in the Sophist tradition cannot consider the nature of God except as a manifestation of what people purport to be responses to the Divine.

This tradition—or some variant of it—is now extremely popular in the "behavioral sciences." It is seen, for example, in the meaning of power which informs American stratification theory in both the Weber and Warner strands. Although an interesting modification of the Sophist view is made by George Herbert Mead and Walter Coutu, two social psychologists who wish to uphold the self-affirming and creative nature of the self, they may be related to this viewpoint.[5]

The fact that the Sophist understanding of power as the ability to attain one's own will in conflict with other wills is comparable to the classical Christian understanding of the power of the fallen man creates a partial convergence between the two groups. Hence, although they invariably introduce other dimensions or considerations, Christian theologians may find the research data presented by persons in this tradition useful at certain levels. An interesting relationship also emerges between representatives of this heritage and Christian theologians, such as Karl Barth, who are skeptical about the ability of human reason to penetrate to the nature of things.

Nevertheless, the Sophist tradition has never been popular among theologians. The unqualified phenomenological character of this approach makes it impossible to understand the nature and character of God in a religiously satisfying manner. Therefore, as noted in the introduction to this chapter, basic disagreements between sociologists informed by this tradition and theologians informed by alternative categorical schema are inevitable.

One of the two approaches which argue for a unity of the sciences has been popular in the Christian heritage; the other is more popular among social scientists. Persons in the Platonic heritage maintain that there are no formal criteria which permit clear-cut distinctions between areas of study. Such differentiations as do emerge are based upon contingent rather than categorical considerations. Because the ultimate unity of the sciences is based upon the systematic interrelatedness and hierarchical ordering of the forms, Platonists characteristically have a strong faith in rationalism. Platonists argue that participation in the same form by different events assures common elements in experience, but they find no reason why all the sciences would focus upon the same subject matter.

The Platonist meaning of freedom differs markedly from the Sophist. Platonists maintain that the free man is ultimately the wise man, the philosopher who has penetrated to the nature of things and grasped the vision of the Good. The language of the ontology informing this tradition is that of harmony and disharmony. The Sophistic understanding of power is only one dimension of the Platonist meaning of power. Because transcendental elements are essential to make sense of immanental ones, God as He is understood in this heritage possesses at least one intrinsic quality.

Most Christian theologians have rejected the Platonic notion that reason can lead man to the Good. Instead, they have insisted that God initiated His revelation of Himself in Jesus Christ. (This appeal to Divine self-initiation of His Revelation is here termed "theo-volitional.") Theologians such as Augustine, Luther, Calvin, Barth, Brunner, H. Richard Niebuhr, and Reinhold Niebuhr, who affirm the dominance of Power or Will in the Divine nature, emphasize the significance of man's experiential confrontation with God transcending form. Although this emphasis, coupled with some doctrine of the fall of man, results in a provisional multiplicity of the sciences, their concept of a God whose reality is authentic and independent of other factors relates them to Plato. This multiplicity of the sciences, based upon man's perspective rather than upon a multiplicity of subject matters, is closer to the Sophistic than the Aristotelian multiplicity.

Immanuel Kant developed the most complex and influential multiplicity of the sciences based on the nature of the observer rather than of the subject matter. He distinguished between the theoretic sciences, in which man's categories of understanding imposed order upon objects in the natural and social world; the practical sciences, in which man's inner moral experience authenticated the reality of human freedom and the Good; and the aesthetic sciences, in which the universal was apprehended in the particular without the use of concepts.

Although not all social scientists in the neo-Kantian tradition articulate a full-blown Kantian categorical scheme, Dilthey, Rickert, Weber, Troeltsch, and their modern successors base their understanding of the social studies on the Kantian distinction between "pure" and "practical" reason. The distinction between statements of fact and statements of value, so popular in this heritage, stands or falls on the adequacy of these Kantian categorical distinctions. This issue will be taken up frequently. It is also characteristic of these social scientists to think that the social sciences should look for configurations and tendencies, but to reject the notion that the social sciences will achieve the degree of precision apparently available in some of the so-called physical sciences.

A further anthropological distinction should be noted. The theologians mentioned above see a propensity toward disharmony internal to man, and thus they tend to order the data of the social world differently from the social scientists just cited. Weber, for example, rejects Kant's ontological dimension and bases value entirely upon self-affirmation. The theologians relate disharmony to the fall and appeal to God's redemptive action in history and personal experience to effect a partial restoration of man's will to God's will.

Variants of Platonic views, particularly the theo-volitional, have been popular among theologians though few contemporary social scientists entertain them. Those neo-Kantians who distinguish between the theoretic and the practical sciences usually do not include the dimension of "revelation," the confrontation of God as will and personality transcending form and matter, which theologians in the Kantian heritage frequently incorporate in their analyses. However some analysts, such as Rudolph Otto in the field of the history of religion, do interpret religious experience in relation to some universal Divine manifestation.

Variations of this transcendental option are explored further in subsequent chapters, especially the first section of Chapter V and Part Four. In the present context, the point deserving emphasis is that this transcendent dimension, however qualified or explicated, constitutes a *sui generis* ground for religious experience, even though it may be only dimly understood and articulated by the individual.

The other perspective affirming a unity of the sciences, presented by Democritus, looks first for underlying elements or components upon which explanations may be posited. The general tendency is to delineate two areas, "science" and "non-science." In the modern period, where the Freudian tradition is representative, consciousness thus tends to become epiphenomenal and to be understood in relation to some basic set of elements. The free man is the one who understands the forces which have made him what he is; this understanding enables him not to transcend these forces but to accept them and live in conformity with them. The pleasure-pain or reward-punishment principle is usually employed to interpret human behavior. This tradition has generally attempted to understand God by referring to forces or elements alleged to have produced notions about Him.

Although the formulations differ in some significant aspects, this pattern is typified by Freud's concept of God as the projection of a father figure and Durkheim's notion of the relation between the conception of God and the social group.[6] The difference centers about the nature of the reality to which the term "God" applies. It is possible to see Durkheim, as a radical phenomenalist, ascribing such a role to society. Both Freud and Durkheim deny a *sui generis* character to the God of religious devotion and explain Him on the basis of their studies. This issue is discussed more fully in Chapter VI.

While most contemporary structural-functional analysis of religion in sociology is related either to this heritage, the Sophistic one, or some amalgam of the two, most theologians have resisted this elemental or atomistic tradition.[7] Such disagreements are to be expected; neither the Sophistic nor the Democritean traditions as expressed in antiquity or as appropriated in the modern period permit appeal to a transcendental dimension which many find necessary to a religiously satisfying understanding of God.

The Aristotelian and Platonic heritages, including significant Christian variations of these traditions, understand religious experience as a confrontation with the ultimate. Although the precise way in which "confrontation with the ultimate" is interpreted depends upon which facet of which tradition is being considered, in all these traditions religion is a response to that which is in some sense ultimate and transcendental. God is viewed neither as a product of more elemental factors nor as an entity to be defined operationally.

The major traditions in the social sciences today consider religion as a function of other phenomena or define it in operational terms. Except for Roman Catholic sociologists, who have founded their own professional society, and a few others, few professional sociologists have appropriated either the Aristotelian or Platonic heritages.[8] For example, the language of balance, harmony, disharmony, of hierarchies of society, of levels of abstraction, of freedom as internal to the organism, and the Platonic ontology to which such language is related seem alien in the social sciences today.

Sociologists affirming Sophistic or Democritean perspectives are most likely to differentiate statements of fact from statements of value and to affirm the "objective" character of science. The nature of the objectivity will differ. For the Sophists, the only kind of objectivity which can be attained is a consensus among workers in the field. For the Democritean view, the objectivity of the scientific enterprise may be insured by careful attention to the method of investigation.

Proponents of these traditions are likely to decry the "Christian Sociology" characteristic of an earlier epoch. Practitioners of "Christian Sociology" were not always clear about the fundamental notions which permitted the use of the term, but Christian social theorists generally wish to see normative dimensions included in social analysis unlike most "secular" sociologists.

In the so-called "liberal" period of Protestant theology, roughly 1880-1930, a significant number of theologians employed basic cognitive structures closely related to those of Democritus or the Sophists, and sociology became widespread in American Protestant theological education. During this time various religious research groups were founded in the United States. Although it had some influence among Roman Catholics, the movement never achieved the widespread popularity there which it attained in American Protestant theological circles. The subsequent decline of this movement undoubtedly contributed to the different climate of opinion which religious researchers encounter today in Protestant theological seminaries and Protestant denominational and interdenominational agencies.

To summarize, the sociologist studying religious phenomena must inevitably become involved in philosophical or theological issues. If he employs the perspectives now dominant in American sociology, his cognitive structures will differ significantly from those in the theological tradition, and disagreement as to the validity of his studies will result.

The Sociologist and Substantive Research

Although the alternate ways of abstracting from the manifold of experience suggested in the previous section may be recognized, it is still necessary to resolve the problem of the use of contingent materials. At this point the social scientist concerned with empirical phenomena may make a special contribution.

This section makes two major presuppositions. First, the formulations reflect a strong rationalistic bias. There is no neutral way to resolve this problem since the critic must also employ some type of cognitive structure open to general appropriation. Even those who reject the possibility of a universal categorical schema affirm the universality of their rejection. Second, the analysis presupposes the validity of the categorical-contingent distinction discussed earlier.

Theologian *qua* theologian and philosopher *qua* philosopher have completed their tasks when they have developed a cognitive structure of universal dimensions. Such a structure is so general that all contingent data, including that relative to a particular sphere, are exemplifications of the categorical schema. Whether such a schema can ever be devised is questionable. In any case, that is the analyst's goal. For example, Reinhold Niebuhr's notion of "man as a part of nature," Paul Tillich's notion of "destiny" as one pole of a basic ontological polarity, and Alfred N. Whitehead's notion of "causal efficacy" suggest that the human organism is conditioned by his environment.[9] The idea of environmental conditioning presupposes man's basic, internal freedom, a concept rejected by some contemporary sociologists. It is important to note that if a sociologist is influenced by any of these thinkers, the direction of his research efforts may be somewhat different.

The above observations are categorical ones, whereas the questions of "How much?" "In what degree?" and "In relation to what structures?" are contingent questions with which a sociologist may deal. The sociologist must take both into account, for the implicit categorical schema employed by the analyst cannot help but condition his research.

Nevertheless, two differences in emphasis seem to be open to those engaged in empirical sociological investigations. The analyst either may employ a fully articulated categorical schema in which to set his data and which, in major part, will direct his research efforts, or he may attempt to present his data at a relatively low level of abstraction, employing relatively neutral categories and undertaking descriptive and typological studies. If the research data are presented at a relatively low level of abstraction, the major problem of using sociological investigations where the investigators have permitted their own schemata to slant or to shape the findings inordinately is minimized, but not eliminated.

If this second approach is followed, the analyst may introduce appropriate normative material whenever it seems necessary or desirable. Although he should explore fact-value issues, he may at times compromise the discussion. This second approach is illustrated in Part Two.

Chapter II

Perspectives on Social Stratification

The hierarchical ordering of human societies has been of perennial interest and has been interpreted in a variety of ways. This chapter explores four aspects of the problem of social stratification.

The nature of elite groups or persons is examined in the following section. The consequences of alternative perspectives on the nature of reality for the interpretation of superordinate-subordinate relationships and for the meaning of freedom are considered. The characterizations permit broad delineations between alternative perspectives, but further explications in specific contexts may be needed because the conditioning effects of alternative methods of analysis upon the understanding of elites are not systematically detailed here.

Contemporary stratification patterns in the United States are discussed in the second section, but no novel empirical data are introduced. Because of an interest in the implications of social stratification for Christianity, a Sophistic schema is used to order the empirical data. As noted in Chapter I, sociological analyses set in this type of informing structure are frequently useful to Christian social theorists because the understanding of power as the ability to attain one's will in conflict with other wills is common to both schemata.

Differing love-justice relations produce different interpretations of these stratification patterns. These alternative theological perspectives are explored in the third section.

The final section presents a constructive interpretation of the implications of social stratification for religious institutions in the United States.

Alternative Conceptualizations of Hierarchical Patterns

There are four pervasive dimensions in human experience: the influence of the past upon the present, the decisions made in the present, the forms of thought and their relation to the world, and the immanence of a transcendent reality. Thinkers emphasize different components; some deny the reality of one or more of these components by explaining them in terms of the others.

Each of these components gives rise to a different perspective on the nature of reality. Two of these understandings posit a "world behind the world" or, at the minimum, a "depth" dimension in experience. The other two interpretations are phenomenological and therefore affirm the ultimate validity of "concrete" experience. Different understandings of the nature of the elite group in a society and of the meaning of freedom and salvation emerge from each of the four perspectives.

In this discussion, the four perspectives are provisionally distinguished from each other. The distinctions are heuristic, though not entirely neutral. Protagonists of some perspectives want to incorporate all of them in a balanced and inclusive whole; protagonists of other perspectives do not. Those who affirm the reality of a "world behind the world," for example, may legitimately hold that this terminology reflects a phenomenological bias and therefore partially distorts reality.

Two approaches may be made by those who believe in a "world behind the world" or some "depth" dimension to experience. They may posit some elemental base which produces or determines the way man feels, thinks and behaves, or they may posit a transcendental reality or a dimension of depth which man experiences and to which he should relate.

In the former case, one will attempt to discover the "laws" of human behavior by examining the forces and factors which have produced man and society. The free man is he who understands the forces and factors which have made him; man is saved by learning to live in conformity with these forces and factors. Scientists or social engineers make up the elite group because they understand the underlying processes or elements which shape human society and man. Two types of law exist: law based on the understanding of underlying forces or processes and law conventional in human society. As it is possible to evolve the notion of simple or elemental parts in several ways, a variety of approaches may designate scientists or engineers as the elite group.

This perspective on the nature of reality has never been fashionable in the Christian tradition. However, the "destiny" facet of man who is related to nature permits Christian analysts to direct attention to some of the causal considerations dominant in this elementalist or reductionist approach. This approach is quite fashionable today in the so-called "behavioral sciences."

In the latter case, an "isness-oughtness" contrast is discerned. Two broad emphases are possible. If one assumes that there are forms, ideas, or eternal objects—as they have been variously called in this transcendental perspective—behind or inextricably related to the events of experience, he will make some distinction between appearance and reality or will discern complex relations between the events of experience and the Divine. The free man is the wise man who has penetrated to or experienced "the Good" and who possesses philosophic wisdom. Two kinds of freedom are posited. The first, self-determination, is inferior to the second, philosophic wisdom arising from the intuition or the experience of an ultimate harmony of harmonies.

Plato suggested that the Sophists possessed the first kind of freedom, while the philosopher-king possessed the second kind. At this highest level freedom and knowledge coincide. In the ideal state, the philosopher-king would perform the ordering, coordinating and harmonizing functions of government. The elite group possesses this philosophic wisdom.

There are also two kinds of law. The law of reason is superior to that law found in the state. Since philosophers are not kings, a perfectly ordered and hierarchical society such as the one Plato envisioned in *The Republic* cannot be realized. In the real world, the inferior law characteristic of states and the hierarchical ordering partially based upon power understood as the ability to achieve one's own will in conflict with other wills are necessary. These power groups are related to elite groups which possess some measure of the higher philosophic wisdom. These elites should be institutionalized in special bodies such as the U.S. Senate and consultative bodies of elders.

Although this perspective has not been popular in the Christian tradition in this relatively pure form, a second transcendental perspective on reality has been fashionable in the Christian tradition. God is understood as will and personality transcending both form and matter. As with the other transcendental perspective, two meanings of freedom and law emerge.

The man who possesses true freedom and who is the true elite is the man who has experienced the redeeming and forgiving character of Divine Love and whose will conforms with the Divine Will; self-centered man has a false freedom. The law of love, the harmony of life with life, is the highest law, but it differs from law in the world.

The relation between this experience of ultimate harmony and the world is interpreted in different ways. These relations are explored in detail in Chapters XI, "The Relation of Religion and Culture: Analytic and Constructive Perspectives," and XII, "Love, Justice and Forms of Social Organization." At the moment, it is sufficient to observe that the disharmony discerned by the contrast between the experience of an ultimate harmony of harmonies and the world may be explained by finitude, ignorance, and/or sin. The first of the two transcendental or depth perspectives bases its explanation of the contrast upon finitude and ignorance, while the second bases its explanation upon finitude, ignorance and sin.

The other two perspectives on the nature of reality are phenomenal. Protagonists do not posit a world behind the world, in any sense "more real" than the reality of phenomena.

In one view, protagonists posit the self-affirming and primary significance of the individual and his perspective. The free man is the man who can do what he wants to do. Absence of external physical restraint is the ultimate criterion of freedom, so the elite group which emerges is the "power" elite. The ordering of social groups and individuals is based on the power which groups or individuals possess. Laws are strictly conventional, depending upon a consensus or the will of the stronger.

As noted previously, this understanding of power bears a tantalizing relationship to Christian understandings.[1] The Sophist perspective makes normative this self-affirming understanding of freedom, but Christian theologians reject this interpretation. They contrast the ordering, harmonizing and coordinating dimensions of experience with this sinful expression of self-love.

This Sophist perspective is extremely fashionable in contemporary social studies. Both the Warner and the Weber analyses of social stratification presuppose this meaning of power. Because this understanding is incorporated within Christian interpretations, empirical investigations of social stratification which employ this meaning of power are useful to many Christian theologians.

In the other phenomenal approach to the nature of social reality, protagonists begin with the concrete situation in which they find themselves. Law is objectively embedded in concrete form in constitutions, individuals, and institutions. Freedom becomes self-realization, so the analyst traces man's choices through social institutions and in social situations. Since experience reveals a multiplicity of subject matters, there is a multiplicity of elites. In politics, the elite group is a political elite which has acquired the skills, experiences, and abilities pertaining to politics.

Political classes are delineated by relations between the ruler and the ruled, so political analysis would examine the processes and distribution of political choices among various groups in a society. Economic classes are delineated by relations to various occupations, so economic analysis would examine the processes of economic activity and the distribution of economic groups in a society. Social classes are delineated by relations to various habits and virtues, so social analysis would examine the values and style of life of various social groups in a society. In any society, the three dimensions would interrelate; social scientific analysis may examine the inter-relations. The delineations permit both descriptive and normative evaluations.

The dominance of form in this perspective encourages the development of rather rigid hierarchical models of social organization and the elaboration of systems of casuistry. Proponents of this perspective also bear tantalizing relations to Christian social theorists, since one of the most significant proponents of this view was Aristotle, who was appropriated and modified by Thomas Aquinas.

The natural hierarchical ordering of society and the elaboration of systems of casuistry in classical Catholic social theory reflect this perspective. In classical Lutheran understanding, the hierarchy is reflected in the "orders of creation." These issues are considered in greater detail in the following section.

Social Stratification and Religious Institutions in the United States

As the voluminous number of investigations attests, social stratification has been one of the major interests of empirically oriented sociologists in the United States for the past generation or so. Because of his emphasis on the importance of will and decisions in human affairs, Max Weber's interpretative schema is useful when ordering and interpreting empirical data on social stratification in the United States. His understanding of power is comparable to the Christian understanding of the power of the sinful man and to the Platonic understanding of the power of the ignorant man. Though Platonic or Christian theorists would hold that his view of power is truncated and overemphasizes conflict, they can use data ordered by his framework.

Weber posited three orders through which power is manifest, although the ultimate referee of power is the individual will. The orders through which power is manifest are the social order, in which dominant style of life is the distinguishing characteristic; the economic order, in which the production and the distribution of goods and materials are the distinguishing characteristics; and the legal order, in which rational rules and regulations are the distinguishing characteristics. Because these characterizations are formal and heuristic, convergences and overlaps occur between the orders in empirical situations.

In the contemporary United States, those who rank high in the social order usually rank high in the economic order and vice versa; therefore, empirical studies of social stratification in the United States which do not distinguish these two components do not distort the situation too markedly. W. Lloyd Warner and his associates have undertaken more studies of social stratification in American society than anyone else. These studies intertwine Weber's conceptions of class, status, and party, but the high correlation between these components just noted minimizes the distortions which such an inclusive schema produces. Even though one may disagree with their conceptual schema, their empirical studies of social stratification may be used profitably.

This section explores the implications of social stratification for religious institutions in the United States. Style of life is very important for such institutions because the type of social interaction characteristic of most American churches usually presupposes a common style of life among members.

Since many of the Warner studies focused upon style of life, it is appropriate to consider them in this chapter. Warner uses class to refer to style of life, while Weber uses status. These differing uses have caused some confusion. In the summary of Warner's delineation of social strata, "class" is employed as Warner uses the term. In the remainder of the discussion the term "status" is used, since the primary interest here, granted the empirical intertwining between class and status in the United States, is the consequences of alternative styles of life for religious institutions.

Warner originally suggested three major social class groupings in the United States which he termed the upper, the middle, and the lower. He further posited two sub-groupings, upper and lower, within each of the major groupings.[2] Although Warner tends to hypostatize what are partially statistical abstractions, his delineations are still useful. His preliminary interpretation of social stratification reveals a Sophistic understanding of power and prestige.

The various strata are differentiated by style of life, prestige and power, associational patterns, fundamental value orientations, source and amount of income, occupation and similar factors related both to the social order and to the economic order. This section presents a brief and over-simplified description of the most crucial characteristics of the various strata. Though this description would have to be refined to be fully adequate, it will suffice here; for the description is developed for use with formulations in the last section of this chapter.

As noted, Warner's strata are partly statistical.[3] It is also evident, both on theoretical and empirical grounds, that differentiations occur within the various strata. Those persons who are upwardly mobile must adopt some values of higher strata; those who are downwardly mobile, some values of lower strata. These facts are important for the churches, since it is highly likely that persons who are classified in the lower strata by some criteria but who participate in the life of main-line Protestant churches are upwardly mobile. One of the consequences of most church membership and participation is the encouragement of a middle or upper class style of life.

The lowest social stratum, which Warner calls the lower-lower class, is the group with the lowest prestige and the least power in a community. The group is characterized by a hand-to-mouth existence and a high percentage of unskilled workers. Work habits tend to be erratic among members of the lower-lower class; many are on some type of public assistance.

Members of the lowest stratum tend to be politically inactive. If they are voters, they are more likely to support the Democratic than the Republican party. Disaffected from the community, they show the most deviation from community mores.

They participate in very few organizational activities, and their family life is apt to be disorganized. This group is culturally disinherited: they read almost no magazines, newspapers or books and tend to reject education and regularized patterns of life. Members of the group have low verbal facilities.

Members of this stratum are most likely to join Pentecostal religious institutions or mission-supported main-line religious institutions. Only a very small segment of this portion of the population participates in any institutional religious life.

Religious professionals who work in areas populated largely by the lowest socio-economic stratum frequently emphasize the intellectual abilities and leadership capacities of the persons with whom they come in contact. Their assessment is probably correct, for it is highly probable that the more able and articulate residents in depressed areas are attracted to religious institutions in disproportionate numbers. Such persons are probably either upwardly mobile, members of a higher social strata than the one dominant in the area, or both. Much more empirical work on value orientations and involvement in religious institutions is needed for a fuller exploration of the issues related to differential involvement in religious institutions by social status.

The next social stratum is the upper-lower class. Financial problems remain strong, but the pattern of life is more regular than that of the lowest stratum. The work habits of members of the upper-lower class are less erratic than those of lower-lower class members, but they are still relatively uneven. A high proportion of the workers are semi-skilled.

Members of this group are most likely to be Democrats. A higher proportion participate in political life and in other voluntary associations than do members of the lowest stratum of society, but their participation is considerably less than that of members of higher strata.

Members of this class frequently display a relatively strong moral legalism or absoluteness. The majority attempt to maintain an orderly family life, and parents frequently want their children to move up in the social scale. The intellectual horizons of members of this group are quite limited, but they do more reading and have somewhat greater verbal facility than most members of the lowest stratum.

As observed earlier, one is apt to discern divergences in style within this broad stratum. Involvement in religious institutions is most likely related to this differentiation. This group and the one above it, which Warner calls the lower-middle class, provide the majority of members of religious institutions.

Members of the lower-middle class are somewhat better off economically than members of either of the lower groups, but their economic concerns remain relatively pressing. Greater differentiation in type of work is characteristic of this group which includes both skilled laborers and white-collar workers. This heterogeneousness suggests that the stratum is more likely to be a statistical abstraction than some of the others. Lower-middle class work habits are quite regularized. This pattern is the rule rather than the exception.

The group is more diverse politically with a higher proportion of Republicans. Participation in voluntary associations, including religious institutions, is considerable, but members of the upper-middle and the upper classes are more involved in a broader range of organizations.

Members of the lower-middle class emphasize the family and "proper" behavior. Some members of this class read popular magazines, but few read books. They possess somewhat more verbal facility than those in lower strata. People in the lower-middle class are apt to affirm the value of education, and they often hope to send their children to college.

The upper-middle class is characterized by considerable power and prestige and by strong organizational participation. The group is comprised of white-collar workers such as professional people, some managerial people, and top salesmen. They have good homes and secure, relatively high incomes.

The group is dominantly Republican. Upper-middle class people are the leaders in a variety of voluntary associations, including religious institutions. The group is relatively exclusive; members of this class interact rather infrequently with those of lower social strata.

Members of the upper-middle class participate in a relatively large number of social functions and parties. They possess organizational and parliamentary know-how, have a high degree of verbal facility, and are strong supporters of professional competence. They place great value in education, and they read more books and magazines than do persons in any other class.

The upper classes possess the greatest degree of prestige and much power. Their base of economic support is beyond question. Many members of the group occupy top-level positions in management and finance, while others have inherited considerable or great wealth.

The upper stratum are strongly Republican. Members of the upper classes belong to more voluntary associations than people in any other stratum, but participate less frequently in religious institutions than upper-middle class groups.

The emphasis upon a special and exclusive style of life is most evident in these groups. Members of the top social stratum, for example, emphasize formal dinners, and, conversely, foster variations and inversions of this ritualized style. They belong to exclusive clubs and organizations which have limited memberships and which screen applicants carefully. Members of the upper strata are concerned about education at prestige institutions. Members presuppose that their peers have traveled extensively and possess an appropriate knowledge of the arts. Differentiation within this top stratum is related to the tradition of the family. Members of the upper classes are patrons of the arts and philanthropies.

The social strata just delineated are distributed unevenly among the religious groups in the United States. As American religious institutions are affected by these status differences, it is important to note the broad patterns. In the United States Roman Catholic churches are the most socially inclusive. Greater differentiations occur in Protestant and Jewish religious institutions. Because of the low percentage of low status Jews, Jewish congregations are dominantly middle and upper status, while differentiations by denomination occur within Protestantism.

Although the major Protestant denominations encompass the entire range of status classifications, the relative distributions differ markedly. The Episcopalians, the Presbyterians, and the Congregational-Christian segment of the United Church of Christ draw disproportionately from upper-middle and upper status populations. The United Methodist church, the Evangelical and Reformed portion of the United Church of Christ, the American Baptists, the Southern Baptists, the Disciples of Christ and the Lutheran bodies draw disproportionately from lower-middle status groups. All of the main-line Protestant denominations have fewer lower status members than does the population as a whole. Pentecostal and Holiness type institutions draw disproportionately from lower and lower-middle status groupings. Local religious institutions do not include as many social strata as their national bodies because a local body generally draws its members from a fairly small and usually homogeneous geographical area.

The pervasive influence of the styles of life characteristic of the various social classes conditions the value orientations of the members of various religious institutions.[4] Because the influences of status and religious affiliation on value orientations are interrelated and reciprocal, it is difficult to determine the relative contributions of the two factors to decision making. These stratification patterns are subject to alternative theological interpretations which will be explored in the following section.

Alternative Theological Interpretations of Hierarchical Patterns

The preceding discussion of social stratification and religious institutions in the United States is an over-simplification and partial distortion, but it may serve as an empirical referee for the analytic and constructive formulations in this and the following sections. An initial problem should be noted. Most of the studies from which these generalizations and characterizations have been drawn were made by analysts who are not informed by either of the transcendental understandings of the nature of reality discussed earlier in this chapter, so unifying elements based upon religious insight are not considered. Most contemporary sociologists either stress conflict between the various strata or advance alternative interpretations to explain the presence of some harmony and cooperation between the various social strata.

C. Wright Mills' early work on social stratification stresses conflict and power struggle between various classes. He minimizes the satisfaction which members of the lower strata find in life and emphasizes the power which elites exercise to dominate others. W. Lloyd Warner sets social differentiation in the context of a harmonizing and integrating whole. He stresses the common participation of all the social strata in American society and cites certain national symbolic events, such as Memorial Day, Independence Day, Veteran's Day, and Thanksgiving, which unify the people of the nation.[5]

Theologians who look to a transcendent harmony to explain the presence of some peace in society may still interpret social stratification in varying ways because they have different conceptions of the relation between perfect harmony and the world. Three broad types of love-world relations guide the theologian's evaluation of stratification patterns.[6]

Protagonists of the first type see a radical disjunction between love and the world, but they respond in two different ways to the disjunction. In the classical Lutheran "two worlds" perspective, the hierarchical ordering of society is related to the "orders of creation." When the Fall disrupted the harmonious natural differentiations of creation, the perfectly harmonious inter-group relations which the Creator intended were also disturbed. Man now experiences conflict and struggle between various groups. He is counseled, for the most part, to endure this situation and to work in the vocation to which he has been called. This counsel has served to support existing patterns. The radical sectarian alternative rejects the fallen world. The elect are counseled to withdraw into an autonomous holy community which will develop more harmonious hierarchical patterns. This counsel has disrupted existing patterns.

Protagonists of the second type of love-world relations see a positive relation between love and the world. Calvinism and Roman Catholicism have both interpreted the stratification of society in an ambiguously positive manner. Although differentiations within human society are inevitable, they may be modified or clarified.

Because of the dominance of form in its social ethics, the Roman Catholic interpretation of social stratification has historically encouraged the development of harmonious relations within rather clear-cut hierarchical patterns. Natural law clarified the relations between classes. The emphasis on the dominance of dynamics in Calvinistic social ethics has modified the hierarchical patterns as Calvinists sought to express their calling through their vocation.

Protagonists of the third type of love-world relations tend to identify one with the other. In the transforming variant, a particular religio-political program is advanced to overcome the disharmony of social stratification; proponents of this point of view often advance utopian and radically egalitarian ideas. In the conserving variant, a present or earlier form of social, political or economic organization is held desirable; proponents usually hold that social stratification is normal and desirable.

Theologians who envision a positive relation between love and the world may interpret current stratification patterns in the United States in an ambiguously positive manner. One such interpretation is advanced in the final section which considers the implications of social stratification for religious institutions.

A Constructive Interpretation

Social stratification is inevitable in all human societies, for it is rooted in man's biological nature and is compounded by man's creating, shaping, and forming capacities. The vision of perfect harmony inherent in one facet of the Divine nature has led some theorists to envision an ideal world in which there is perfect harmony of life with life. This world is contrasted with the real world in which disharmonious dimensions are intertwined with harmonious ones. The Christian idea of a perfection before the Fall, the stoic doctrine of a Golden Age, and the Platonic view of the perfectly hierarchically ordered and coordinated state all reflect such a vision and make such contrasts.

This contrast confuses potentiality with actuality. The experience of the lure for harmony is part of human experience, but finitude and ignorance preclude the realization of perfect harmony.[7] The disharmony induced by social stratification may be minimized, but it cannot and should not be eliminated. The contributions of all of the parts to the harmony of a functioning whole are the positive aspects of social stratification and differentiation; exploitation and mediocrity are the negative aspects. Current stratification patterns in the United States should be supported with certain qualifications. Two of the principles of justice, equality appropriate to form and self-determination informed by excellence, lead to this evaluation.

The greatest distortions of man's humanity occur in the lowest social stratum, since a measure of political, social and economic equality and self-determination informed by excellence are part of humanness. The economic needs of those in the lowest social stratum limit sharply the potentiality which they may realize. These needs may be substantially reduced in affluent nations by a proper welfare policy which extends a measure of equality to members of this group and simultaneously sustains the vision of self-determination informed by excellence. Persons in the top social strata are especially tempted either to minimize equality, to assert self-determination excessively, or both.

The relatively open character of social strata in the United States and the opportunities for self-determination informed by excellence in all of them mean that the stratification patterns themselves should not be radically criticized. Religious institutions whose adjustive and integrative activities sustain these patterns are engaging in practices which may be interpreted in an ambiguously positive manner.

The extensive criticism of suburban church life and of middle status style of life which is so fashionable among some American theologians and social critics must be challenged. In part, it is appropriate for religious institutions to support middle status style of life. Although there is a need to institutionalize different styles of church membership and to extend self-conscious theological understanding among laymen in all social strata, the positive latent consequences of current patterns of church life in America for wholesome human interaction, for the support of a monogamous family structure, for the encouragement of a democratic political order, and for the development of persons able to sustain a rational and highly technical economic system should also be accentuated.

Some religious professionals have spent considerable time and money developing programs to foster more intensive inter-strata social interaction between members of religious institutions. These efforts are informed by some vision of the unity of people in the love of Christ, but this unity needs to be balanced by some diversity.

Although the religious professional may encourage closer inter-personal relations between persons separated by several strata among those few who desire such relations, interaction between members of American religious institutions will continue to be largely between members of the same social stratum and ethnic group. The inability of the churches to foster the widespread practice of inter-strata and inter-racial interaction is not necessarily a degradation of the religious institution.

It is extremely difficult for main-line Protestant churches to function in geographical areas dominated by the lowest social stratum. This difficulty is frequently compounded by racial differences. The sharp contrast in style of life between most main-line Protestant religious professionals and the indigenous population of such areas produces very subtle super-ordinate sub-ordinate relations. Although it is possible to transcend these status differentiations, serious misperceptions of the relations between persons in different social strata will occur if the differentiations are ignored. Main-line Protestant churches which do function in such areas are almost always small and partially supported by mission funds. Social service work, highly specialized ministries to institutions, and the further training of indigenous religious professionals may serve as alternatives to direct main-line Protestant ministries in these areas. The professional development of indigenous religious leaders is especially important since no area in the United States is without some type of indigenous religious institution.

Protestant-sponsored social service work has been adversely affected in recent years by two factors. Some religious professionals have questioned church support of social service agencies independent of worshipping communities. Others have urged moral and financial support to organizations which promote direct economic and political action. This situation is lamentable. If the theoretical understanding guiding practice of social service workers is compatible with Christian perspectives, church-sponsored social service work is entirely appropriate. It is especially important that such service supplement government-sponsored programs and respond flexibly to needs which may be unmet by state-supported agencies.

In upper-lower status areas, main-line Protestant religious institutions can function, though they have considerable difficulty maintaining themselves. The dominant forms of religious expression in the major Protestant denominations are most appropriate among the middle and upper social strata. The fuller development of self-conscious theological understanding among upper-middle status members is most urgent, for more people in this stratum are capable of understanding alternative theological perspectives.

The concern with lay adult theological education has become rather general within American Protestantism since the Second World War. Denominational and interdenominational projects, centers, and institutes to foster lay understanding abound. Unfortunately, many of the professionals directing them are critical of the existing forms of the church and hold love-justice views which lead to negative or ambiguously negative interpretations of American society. Some may hope that alternative views may become more prevalent. The constructive portions of this book represent one attempt to foster more sympathetic interpretations of the mainstream of American life.

Chapter III

Alternative Methodological Approaches to Urbanization and Urbanism[1]

Although some of the substantive factors remain more or less at the level of "brute facts," the characterization of a city, the diagnosis of its problems, the suggested solutions to these problems, the interpretation of its contributions to human culture and civilization, and the nature of its relation to individuals and to other political entities are conditioned by an analyst's methodological approach. This chapter delineates alternative methods of sociological analysis of urbanization and urbanism. This focus obscures some dimensions further differentiating analysts who possess comparable methods of analysis but entertain different understandings of the nature of reality. These differences are discussed briefly although the primary emphasis is upon the consequences of alternative methods of sociological analysis for the study of urban life.

Four broad methodological approaches to the study of urban life are possible. Two of them have been used widely by social scientists, while the other two approaches have been used more commonly by Christian social theorists. In this discussion of the methods of analysis, illustrated by references to classical or contemporary writers, the four approaches are related to and contrasted with Christian perspectives.

Even though this chapter deals with alternative methodological approaches to the sociological study of cities, the same broad alternatives are employed in the sociological study of religious phenomena. This matter is explored in Part Three, where a constructive perspective is developed in relation to critiques of Emile Durkheim, Max Weber, and Talcott Parsons.

Dialectical Analysis

Dialecticians synthesize contrasts and apparent opposites at higher levels of abstraction or complexity. Some dialecticians, such as Plato, give ontological status to the concepts which are abstracted from experience; others, such as Max Weber, do not. Dialecticians are usually sensitive to the configuration of factors which produce a unique, complex historical whole because a whole is more than the sum of its parts. The intrinsic inter-relatedness of the parts of a whole limits the extent and value of cross-cultural comparisons in the social sciences. Historical analysis explores the way in which component parts unite to form a unique whole. Because some components are common to all human experience, some cross-cultural and inter-epochal comparisons can be made, but these comparisons are always contrasted with the unique aspects of an historical configuration.

Max Weber uses dialectical analysis in his development of ideal types. He deals with the problem of particularity and generality by distinguishing between non-repeatable and repeatable ideal types. On the one hand, ideal types such as "capitalism" and "patrician city" are non-repeatable because the peculiar complex of factors which contributed to the historical approximations of these types probably will not occur again. On the other hand, ideal types such as "charismatic leader" and "war lord" are repeatable because the factors which contributed to the emergence of historical approximations of these types occur again and again.

In the investigation of particular phenomena, Weber employs contextual analysis, which is discussed in the next section of this chapter. He orders the interplay between conflicting individual and collective wills by crucial structural elements rooted in human consciousness and by ideal types.[2] In his classic book, *The City,* Weber uses this approach to develop a typology of cities.[3] He focuses upon different status, economic and political configurations and upon different cultural conditions to delineate various types of cities. Weber's definition of power as the ability to attain one's individual or collective will in conflict with other wills reflects this interplay. A city is ultimately based upon its ability to exercise its own will in conflict with others, so political autonomy is Weber's salient criterion for the existence of a city. Don Martindale comments on this interpretation in his introduction to the translation of *The City* :

Max Weber's theory of the city, thus, leads to a rather interesting conclusion. We can grant the phenomenal increase and aggregation of modern populations as a concomitant of the industrial revolution. We should not, however, confuse physical aggregation with the growth of the city in a sociological sense. The urban community has everywhere lost its military integrity—its right to defend itself by military means. In many areas of the world it has, temporarily at least, lost its very legal and political autonomy—the same fate is possible everywhere. Meanwhile, within the city itself greater masses of residents pursue interlocal interests—as representatives of the national government, as agents in business and industries of the national government, as agents in business and industries of the national and international rather than of civic scope.

The modern city is losing its external and formal structure. Internally, it is in a state of decay while the new community represented by the nation everywhere grows at its expense. The age of the city seems to be at an end.[4]

Many Protestant social theorists who use a dialectical method of analysis find Weber's sociological analyses useful, though they usually incorporate ontic dimensions which Weber rejects. God as Will and Personality transcending form and personality is the One to Whom man should relate for the contemporary Protestant theologian Reinhold Niebuhr, who is illustrative of theologians in the Pauline-Augustinian-Reformation tradition.[5] God is the ultimate source of harmony. The disharmony experienced in the earthly city is due to man's sinfulness; man has willfully turned away from the source of his existence and has disrupted the harmony of creation.

This understanding of God as the ultimate source of harmony produces an isness-oughtness contrast in Niebuhr's interpretation which is absent in Weber's analyses. Niebuhr contrasts the "earthly city" with the "city of God." Differentiations within the "earthly city" are produced by natural forms and processes and by acts of will.

Weber's meaning of power as the ability to attain one's own will in conflict with others is comparable to Niebuhr's meaning of power for the sinful man so the ultimate basis for the city is similar for the two theorists. For each, the city is a political unit which can exercise its own will. Niebuhr, however, also emphasizes the positive nature of the co-ordinating and harmonizing functions of government, a motif absent in Weber.

Contextual Analysis

Contextual analysis also examines the contrast of opposites and the interplay of forces, but, unlike dialectical analysis, it does not seek to resolve them into a higher unity. The Sophists employed contextual analysis; sociologists today use it under such rubrics as operationalism, contextualism and interactionalism.

Maurice Stein employs a contextual approach in the early portions of his book on cities, *The Eclipse of Community*.[6] He summarizes his approach in this passage:

> This means that every community study is to be viewed as a case study. We can go even further and maintain they should all be studies of the effects of basic processes and historical events on changing social patterns. This means that the state of affairs before the change as well as while it is in progress should be carefully specified. Every good community study is a study of transitional processes.
>
> .   .   .   .   .
>
> It is also worth noting that this model presumes that the theoretical accumulation will pivot around growing insight into the processes of change in various contexts. Instead of searching for representative cases, the query will always be, "What does the case under scrutiny represent?" At the present state of our knowledge, we cannot legitimately assume knowledge of the social structure of any community before beginning research. . . . Our set of structural models can be used to provide clues as to significant groupings but not as a handbook of the range of possibilities. It will take a great deal more research before such a comprehensive handbook can be made available and one can be certain that any such handbook will always be liable to obsolescence as novel patterns emerge. The interpretive focus has to be on the changing configuration and the social processes underlying the observed changes.
>
> This kind of analysis has been called "field-theoretical" by Kurt Lewin. . . . The main point is the recognition that every community can be viewed as an organized system standing in a determinate relationship to its environment. The system-environment model then focuses attention on this relationship between the two. If the research is directed at changing patterns, then the sources of systemtic disorganization, whether internal or environmental, must be carefully examined along with the mechanisms of reorganization.[7]

Using this approach, Stein suggests that the environmental pressures created by urbanization, industrialization and bureaucracy are crucial for the interpretation of contemporary communities in the United States.

Although the absence of transcendent dimensions in the contextualist approach leads most Christian theorists to criticize its truncated character, the contextualist emphases upon specificity and particularity and upon the emergent character of factors conditioning human behavior possess similarities to some Christian perspectives. The structural components used by contextualists may appear fuzzy and inadequate from dialectical perspectives, but most dialecticians find the contextualist's empirical studies useful.

Analysis of Components

The analysis of components represents a third major perspective on urbanization and urbanism. The analyst begins with a set of simple elements or components from which he constructs a set of rigorously interrelated propositions. The development of clear, unequivocal definitions of the objects under investigation is typical for theorists using this approach. The definitions frequently delineate the elements or components which constitute the object of investigation. These elements or components are called independent variables; other elements or components are called dependent variables. Investigators hope that knowledge of changes in a set of independent variables will enable them to predict the corresponding changes in a set of dependent variables. This approach to the study of cities is the most mechanistic and deterministic of the four.

Louis Wirth uses this approach in his famous essay "Urbanism as a Way of Life."[8] In contrast to Stein, Wirth does seek a representative city which may be identified by certain elements or components.

Wirth begins by identifying a set of elements or units which will allow a definition of a city. He then constructs a set of unified propositions which relate to the original set. The interplay between these elements and other identifying characteristics will enable him to arrive at the essential propositions comprising a theory of urbanism. Wirth argues that it is possible to identify the essential determinants of a city independent of an historical context.

> While urbanism, or that complex of traits which makes up the characteristic mode of life in cities, and urbanization, which denotes the development and extensions of these factors, are thus not exclusively found in settlements which are cities in the physical and demographic sense, they do, nevertheless, find their most pronounced expression in such areas, especially in metropolitan cities. In formulating a definition of the city it is necessary to exercise caution in order to avoid identifying urbanism as a way of life with

any specific locally or historically conditioned cultural influences which, while they may significantly affect the specific character of the community, are not the essential determinants of its character as a city.

It is particularly important to call attention to the danger of confusing urbanism with industrialism and modern capitalism. The rise of cities in the modern world is undoubtedly not independent of the emergence of modern power-driven machine technology, mass production, and capitalistic enterprise. But different as the cities of earlier epochs may have been by virtue of their development in a preindustrial and precapitalistic order from the great cities of today, they were, nevertheless, cities.[9]

Wirth ends this section of his essay with a definition of the city. The definition concludes a review of the various elements which are needed in it.

For sociological purposes a city may be defined as a relatively large, dense, and permanent settlement of socially heterogeneous individuals. On the basis of the postulates which this minimal definition suggests, a theory of urbanism may be formulated in the light of existing knowledge concerning social groups.[10]

The interplay between theory and empirical research increases the clarity of the essential propositions. Wirth discusses this procedure later in the essay:

In the pages that follow we shall seek to set forth a limited number of identifying characteristics of the city. Given these characteristics we shall then indicate what consequences or further characteristics follow from them in the light of general sociological theory and empirical research. We hope in this manner to arrive at the *essential propositions* comprising a theory of urbanism.[11]

This perspective is in greater conflict with Christian perspectives than any of the other approaches to the study of cities. The reductionism inherent in the search for an essential city contrasts with alternative whole-part relations envisioned by the other approaches. The mechanistic and deterministic understanding of human life suggested by the search for the laws governing urban life contrasts with alternative ideas of human freedom contained in the other viewpoints.

If research workers using the analysis of components approach present their findings at a relatively low level of abstraction, the data are useful to persons guided by other perspectives. However, as many workers using this approach consider such a presentation naive and unsophisticated, they rarely present their findings in this way. From other perspectives, their refusal to present findings at low levels of abstraction means that they permit their framework to bend their original data inordinately.[12]

Situational Analysis

The situational analyst differentiates the sciences by type of subject matter. The social sciences study the actions of men in human associations, a subject matter which distinguishes them from the aesthetic or the theoretical sciences.

Situational analyses studies the place of the city as it is embedded concretely in a network of human associations. Aristotle used this approach in the *Politics,* where he established a reflective relation between the individual, the family, the household, the village (the city, in modern terms), and the state. Each component is seen in its appropriate relation to each of the other components. The individual has his proper and appropriate relation with the family. The family has its proper and appropriate relation with the household. The household has its proper and appropriate relation with the village. The village has its appropriate and proper relation with the state. Since the relations terminate there, the end of the state is to foster the happiness of the others.

This approach permits an analyst both to study and to evaluate existing forms of social organization. For example, this perspective allows an analyst to examine various forms of family organization and to affirm monogamy as the most desirable form of family organization. Similarly, in an examination of the various relations between the economic and political spheres, he may suggest the desirability of some separation between the two. Because the end of the state is the promotion of the social good, it is appropriate for it to regulate the economic order, but it should not absorb it.

The various components of the social order are examined and evaluated according to their functions. To study the city is to consider the specific functions it performs. Therefore, to identify the city an analyst would look directly at its educational activities, its public safety units such as police and fire departments, its taxation policies, its public services, and its political organization. Just as the aim of the state is to enhance the common good, so the political leadership of the city should enhance the life of its residents by contributing the facilities appropriate to its functions. The study of politics and political organization is especially crucial in an examination of the city.

Because of Roman Catholicism's relation to Aristotle, these formulations continue to be significant. Pope John XXIII's encyclical *Mater et Magistra* is ordered in accord with a situational analysis. The discussion of the various components of the social order begins with the family, the fundamental and elemental cell to which all other components are related. The encyclical affirms a principle of subsidiarity: the smallest component in the social order which can effectively perform a given task should be encouraged to undertake it. This principle allows for changes in the functions of components in different historical epochs; changes in circumstances may result in shifts in functions so that given tasks may be performed effectively. For example, changes in the scale of social organization have shifted the responsibility for education from the family to larger units in the modern period. Similarly, functions once performed by a village or a city, such as military defense, are now functions of the state.[13]

Situational analysis emphasizes reciprocal relations between the individual and social institutions. The effects of institutions upon the habits of men and the effects of men's choices upon the structure of social institutions are examined. Neither is reduced to the other, but the emphasis is upon the forms to which human choices are related. This pattern is the inverse of contextual analysis which emphasizes human decisions. Both seek tendencies and configurations in human behavior, but neither expects to attain the degree of precision for which proponents of the analysis of components hope. The emphasis upon form makes situational analysis more attractive to Catholic social theorists than to Protestant thinkers who find the contextual emphasis upon dynamics more appealing. Both disagree sharply with the analysis of components.

PART TWO

Empirical Applications

Chapter IV

Lay Expectations of the Ministerial Role: an Exploration of Protestant-Catholic Differentials[1]

This chapter is divided into three major sections. The theoretical schema is explicated in the first section. The middle section outlines the design of the study and describes the geographical areas from which the data were drawn. The third section analyzes the findings in terms of the schema developed in the first section. All the findings are presented at a low or a moderate level of abstraction to minimize the differences between various theoretical approaches to the study of religious phenomena. There is no constructive effort to explore the grounds upon which a unity of the multiplicity of qualities ascribed to the religious professional here might be established.

The Point of View

The full-time religious professional associated with a religious institution occupies a strategic position in the social system in which he is involved professionally.[2] The multifarious tasks in which he engages reflect the diffuseness of his responsibilities. This diffuseness is characteristic of leadership roles in any social system, because the coordinating and harmonizing facets of any leadership role demand a generalized role definition.[3]

Although this diffuseness is characteristic of any leadership role, the objectives of the social system which sustains the full-time religious professional are themselves more diffuse and less amenable to rational evaluation than are the goals of most organizations in this society. On its own terms the Christian Church exists to cure and save souls and to witness to God's revelation of His nature in Jesus as the Christ, so its ultimate goal transcends moral, cognitive or emotive goals or objectives. At the same time, moral, cognitive and emotive dimensions are included in the objectives of the Church and in the theological understanding which informs these goals.

The theological difficulties encountered when the Church is treated as a social system are not considered systematically in this chapter. As this discussion does not incorporate transcendent factors which proponents of various perspectives would include, some interpretors will want to re-shape and re-formulate portions of the theoretical parts of this analysis. Many theologians will find the delineation of the components included in the religious professional's role especially suspect. The empirical findings are deliberately presented at a relatively low level of abstraction so that they may be used by persons informed by different theoretical perspectives.

Three major components in the religious professional's role are defined by his activities. The first, an instrumental or technical component, arises because the religious professional in a local religious institution is responsible to a greater or lesser degree for maintaining appropriate facilities in which to conduct the church's activities. He must also support an ecclesiastical bureaucracy extending beyond the local religious institution. Administrative and technical competence are the requisite qualities for this component of a religious professional's role.

The second major component is an emotive or feeling-tone component in which affective and sustaining elements are dominant. Pastoral work, such as calling, counseling and group activities, and the ability to relate well to others are included in this aspect. This component accentuates personal and social integrative and harmonizing tasks.

The last major component in a religious professional's role is religious, which is divisible into cognitive, trans-cognitive, and mixed elements. The cognitive element comprises the teaching tasks of the religious professional. The trans-cognitive element includes the administration of the sacraments and those aspects of the worship service in which music and liturgy are dominant. The mixed element incorporates the preaching function of the full-time religious professional, which includes both cognitive and trans-cognitive dimensions.

This description of the components is largely formal, but some substantive factors are included because the components have been delineated operationally. Some theological perspectives regard all of the components as interrelated and manifestations of the religious component. If this chapter were a constructive one, the material would be so ordered, but the intent here is to interpret the consequences of different lay expectations of the components in a religious professional's role.[4]

The Design of the Study and the Locale

The findings in this chapter are based on data drawn from a larger study undertaken in a Corn Belt county.[5] Data gathered in two towns in Corn County are compared and contrasted. In one of the communities, called Maizeville here, about seventy percent of the adults were Protestant, about ten percent were Catholic, and about twenty percent were not church members. In the other town, called East Town here, about twenty percent of the adults were Protestant, about sixty percent were Catholic, and about twenty percent were not church members. Maizeville is a county seat town of about six thousand; East Town is an industrial town of about five thousand adjacent to a larger industrial complex of about thirty thousand.

There were thirteen Protestant churches and one geographically defined Catholic parish in Maizeville. There was one Anglo-European origin Protestant church, one Syrian Orthodox church, and four nationality defined Roman Catholic parishes in East Town. Because of migration and intermarriage there is now considerable ethnic diversity in all of these Catholic parishes so Catholic laymen in East Town have some choice of parish. Minority-majority status in a community and the number of churches from which laymen may choose are additional conditioning factors which might effect lay expectations of the religious professional's role in the two towns.

A twenty-five percent sample of all adult church members except Methodists was drawn in Maizeville. Adults were defined as single persons over twenty years and married persons of any age. Only a twelve and one-half percent sample of Methodists was drawn because of their greater numerical frequency. The data for Protestants have not been adjusted for this differential, but the burden of the analysis would not be changed, as the pattern of Methodist responses was very close to the pattern of all Protestant responses. A six and one-quarter percent sample of Roman Catholics and a sixteen and two-thirds percent sample of Protestants was drawn in East Town. Responses from two questions in the Corn County interview schedule are examined in the following section.

The Findings

Table 1 presents data on the qualities or characteristics which respondents valued most highly in a religious professional. Those who were members of denominations whose polity permitted it were asked to imagine that they were members of a pulpit committee looking for a new minister. They were then asked to indicate the qualities or characteristics they would consider most important. Others were simply asked to indicate their judgment about the most important qualities or characteristics of a new minister (or priest). The total number of qualities cited exceeded the number of respondents in each category due to multiple responses.

The relevant responses have been categorized under the three main components of the religious professional's role developed in the first section of this chapter. Responses which were non-substantive or which cited ascribed characteristics are not considered here.

The first major component, religious, includes citations referring explicitly to the religious professional's responsibilities in the conduct of public worship. The second major component, emotive, includes responses citing qualities of affective feelings and interpersonal relations. The last major component, instrumental, includes responses referring to the administrative competence of the religious professional.

As Table 1 reveals, the emotive or affective dimension was cited most frequently. Two of the three elements of the religious component were cited rather frequently, but technical or instrumental administrative qualities were rarely cited. The strong emphasis among both Catholics and Protestants on the emotive component contrasts sharply with the dominance of cognitive and instrumental components in other facets of contemporary American society. More than half of the qualities cited in each group examined here were in this component. The most frequent single response by far was that the professional religious leader should "be able to get along with people."

This finding highlights the integrative and adjustive functions expected of the religious professional in American society. Conversely, the prophetic and critical functions of the religious professional are not strongly institutionalized at the local level. The findings also suggest that technical and administrative tasks are not highly valued by laymen, even though they occupy a significant segment of the religious professional's time.[6]

The data suggest that the more clearly delineated role definition of the Catholic religious professional stabilizes his role somewhat. Considerably fewer expectations per respondent were cited by Roman Catholics than by Protestants in both East Town and Maizeville. Although the data are not reported here, this relationship remained when the data were controlled for status differentials. As one would expect, Protestants placed a greater emphasis upon the sermon, which is categorized as a mixed component because it incorporates both cognitive and trans-cognitive elements.

Except for these differences, lay expectations for Protestant and Catholic religious professionals were similar. Common expectations are certainly as or more significant than the differences which emerge between the two groups.[7]

No layman mentioned the administration of the sacraments or the performance of rites of passage which are included under the transcognitive religious element. The absence of such a reference may mean one of three things. First, respondents may have considered it so pervasively significant that it was not cited. Second, respondents may actually have had little interest in the sacraments. Third, the question which was asked may not have suggested a response in this area. A consideration of related questions leads to the conclusion that the low number of citations does reflect lay disinterest and apathy toward the sacraments.

An increase in the number of Catholic churches from which a layman may choose did not increase the emphasis on the personal adjustive qualities of the religious professional. Slightly more Catholic respondents in East Town than in Maizeville cited this quality, but the number of responses per respondent was markedly less in industrial East Town than in service center Maizeville.

Although not presented here, the data were analyzed by social status using occupation, level of education, and house type as criteria of social status. Two groups were employed in the analysis. The first group consisted of persons in white-collar occupations with at least a high school education who lived in average or better houses. The other group consisted of blue-collar workers with a high school education or less who lived in average or worse houses. The house type scale was the one used by W. Lloyd Warner and his associates.[8] More qualities were cited by the white-collar group than by the blue-collar group for both Protestants and Catholics, but the rank order of qualities cited was the same as in Table 1 for all the groupings examined.

The second question considered here explored the expected conduct of the religious professional. Respondents were asked if they thought a minister or priest should conduct himself differently than other people in a community. A Protestant-Catholic differential would suggest that laymen affirmed the difference in understanding of the religious profes-

TABLE 1. Types of Qualities Expected in Professional Religious Leadership in Percent of Qualities Cited for Protestants and Catholics: Maizeville and East Town.

		Type of Quality							
		Religious			Emotive		Personal "Adjustive" Qualities	Instru-mental[a]	Average No. of Qualities per Respondent
Church Membership of Respondent	N =	Trans-cognitive[a]	Mixed	Cogni-tive[a]	Pastoral Work Ind.[a]	Group[a]			
MAIZEVILLE									
Catholic	52	0	17	7	14	3	57	1	1.33
Protestant	487	0	24	7	7	9	51	2	2.11
EAST TOWN									
Catholic	102	0	9	3	18	0	67	3	1.17
Protestant	57	0	19	11	8	5	56	1	1.47

Maizeville: $X^2 = 1.7536$ $.30 < P < .50$
East Town: $X^2 = 3.555$ $.10 < P < .20$

[a] Columns combined in chi square analysis.

sional's role which is made theologically between Catholics and Protestants. Responses might also reflect the respondent's attitude toward certain norms in society symbolized by the behavior of the religious professional.

As Table 2 indicates, there was a very close agreement between Protestant and Catholic laymen in Maizeville, but marked divergence occurred in East Town. In this heavily Catholic industrial community, the overwhleming majority of Catholics affirmed a distinction consistent with a sharp lay-professional role differentiation. Although the findings are not shown here, an analysis of the responses by social status indicated that the differences could not be accounted for by this variable.

There were sufficient cases in Maizeville to explore this phenomenon further. Table 3 shows the distribution of the responses to this question by intellectual ability and by type of church membership. Intellectual ability was obtained from the interpretation of TAT records which were gathered as a part of the total interview. Persons who scored above average on either intellectual functioning or imaginative ability were placed in the above average group. Persons who scored below average on either factor were placed in the below average group. The remainder were placed in the average group.

In this study, frequency of attendance has been used to distinguish type of church membership. Persons who considered themselves church members were classed as follows: (A) Dormant: had not attended church in the year prior to the interview. (B) Marginal: had attended church one to eleven times in the year prior to the interview. (C) Modal: had attended church twelve to forty times in the year prior to the interview. (D) Nuclear: had attended church forty-one times or more in the year prior to the interview.

The largest proportion of respondents who made no distinction between lay and ministerial conduct were among dormant and marginal members of average and below average intelligence. It is reasonable to infer that these persons are most isolated from the churches and are most likely to incorporate patterns of behavior and value orientations which deviate from those most highly valued in the community. As these values are symbolized by the behavior expected of the religious professional, the relatively strong distinctions may reflect their resentment of the norms of personal conduct dominant in the community.

The persistence of lay-clergy behavior contrasts and the emphasis upon adjustive and integrative clergy behavior dominate these findings and require further consideration. Although it is beyond the scope of this

TABLE 2.   Conduct Expected of Professional Religious Leadership in Percent for Protestants and Catholics: Maizeville and East Town.

Conduct Expected

Church Membership	N =	No Lay-Professional[a] Distinction Verbalized	Christian-Non-Christian[a] Distinction Verbalized	Lay-Professional Distinction Verbalized
		MAIZEVILLE		
Catholic	51	22	2	76
Protestant	483	22	8	70
		EAST TOWN		
Catholic	96	4	0	96
Protestant	57	30	2	68
Maizeville:	$X^2 = 0.6929$	$.30 < P < .50$		
East Town:	$X^2 = 21.8331$	$P < .001$		
	$C = .35$			

[a] Columns combined in chi square analysis.

chapter to consider in detail the differences within the Christian tradition, it is necessary to develop some dimensions of the dominant Christian value orientations and to contrast these with the value orientations prevalent in contemporary American society in order to understand these findings more adequately.

Though there are significant differences between Protestant and Catholic approaches to social ethics, both traditions affirm the value of the human person.[9] Their emphasis upon love of God and love of neighbor as central values leads to the belief that in many contexts a person should be treated as an end himself rather than as a means to the achievement of other ends. In contrast, the technical rationalism which has contributed to the industrialization, bureaucratization, and urbanization dominating contemporary America has highlighted the use of human beings as means to achieve ends. Roles are rather sharply defined, and technical skills are emphasized.

These two emphases are not mutually exclusive, but they cannot be completely harmonized. Elements in the first value complex are emphasized in Christian ethics while elements in the latter are dominant in contemporary America.[10] The latter complex finds sharpest focus in the values which sustain the modified capitalistic enterprise economic system of the United States.

Since human beings are evaluated by criteria of technical competence and are circumscribed in their social relations by rather clear-cut definitions of proper limited relations with others in the economic sphere, they seek areas in which more wholistic and emotive relations can be maintained. For some, the church provides such an area; hence the lay emphasis upon adjustive and integrative behavior helps explain the opposition which religious professionals encounter when they attempt to exercise a prophetic function in a local church, for such a function is not only disruptive but is also partly incompatible with the leadership responsibilities of a religious professional in that situation. Prophetic functions, therefore, are more easily exercised by religious professionals in an ecclesiastical bureaucracy or a theological school. Priestly functions which sustain and conserve are dominant in local religious institutions.

The contrasts between some of the values pervasive in American society and some of the values dominant in Christian theology help explain the contrasts between lay and professional standards of conduct which the respondents maintained. The religious professional is expected to be a model of conduct for laymen. Because religious professionals in a local religious institution are better able to relate to the personal needs of

TABLE 3.   Conduct Expected of Professional Religious Leadership in Percent by Intellectual Ability and Type of Church Membership: Maizeville.

Conduct Expected

Church Membership	N=	No Lay-Professional[a] Distinction Verbalized	Christian-Non-Christian[a] Distinction Verbalized	Lay-Professional Distinction Verbalized
		Aver. Intellectual Ability		
Dormant & Marginal	88	44	5	51
Modal & Nuclear	148	19	5	76
		Above Aver. Intellectual Ability		
Dormant & Marginal	20	5	5	90
Modal & Nuclear	94	4	11	85
		Below Aver. Intellectual Ability		
Dormant & Marginal	22	45	5	50
Modal & Nuclear	44	23	7	70

Average Intellectual Ability: $X^2 = 14.9152$ $P < .001$ $C = .24$
Above Average Intellectual Ability: $X^2 = .6726$ $.30 < P < .50$
Below Average Intellectual Ability: $X^2 = 2.6532$ $.10 < P < .20$

[a] Columns combined in chi square analysis.

others, they may embody a style of life which laymen feel is more compatible with a Christian ethic than their own.[11]

Summary and Conclusions

The diffuseness of all leadership roles suggests that no person occupying a leadership role in a local religious institution can avoid fulfilling religious, emotive, and instrumental responsibilities even though lay expectations of the religious professional's role focus most strongly upon personal adjustive and integrative qualities. Technical professional competence, either cognitive or administrative, is not highly valued by laymen, but the religious professional must possess such qualities.

The diffuse role definition and the affective qualities cited by laymen contrast with the particularistic role definition and the instrumental qualities dominant in contemporary American society. This lay valuation emphasizes the integrative and adjustive role of the religious professional, and it helps explain the difficulties religious professionals in most local churches encounter when they try to exercise prophetic functions.

The stronger institutionalization of the religious professional's role in the Roman Catholic tradition is reflected in some differences in role expectation between Catholic and Protestant respondents. All Catholic respondents cited a lower average number of expected qualities, and East Town Catholics contrasted lay-professional conduct expectations more strongly than Protestants. These Catholic-Protestant differences should not be exaggerated for they are balanced by tendencies toward a common understanding. For example, if the qualities are ranked in order of the number of times they were cited by respondents, the Catholic and Protestant rankings are comparable.

The persistence of lay-professional distinctions in behavior, which is supported by some of the contrasts between the religious traditions and the American ethos, is reflected in the data. The majority of laymen in all of the examined groups affirmed the distinction. A larger proportion of East Town Catholics maintained the distinction, while the difference between Catholics and Protestants in dominantly Protestant Maizeville was negligible. These findings suggest that the sharpness of lay-professional contrasts are modified by ethnicity, social status, and minority-majority relations. Nevertheless, lay expectations of differences in conduct are pervasive among all groups and should not be ignored by the religious professional.

Chapter V

Protestant Involvement in Community Organizations with Special Reference to The Woodlawn Organization

The analysis in this chapter is guided by an informing perspective other than those currently fashionable in sociology. Material which many sociologists would classify as normative, analytic and empirical are deliberately intertwined in this discussion of the proper relation of Protestant churches to community organizations and agencies. Although the issue is a general one, it is here considered in relation to a particular community organization. The Woodlawn Organization is taken as a prototype of community organizations informed by an organizational theory and strategy with which a large number of religious institutions will have to deal in the next decade or two.

The Woodlawn Organization is a highly controversial militant community organization located on the south side of Chicago in the Woodlawn community area. Woodlawn is overwhelmingly Afro-American and a high proportion of its population receives some type of public assistance. The area would be characterized as depressed by any socio-economic criteria which might be applied.

The Woodlawn Organization was launched with the assistance of the Industrial Areas Foundation, whose organizational techniques it employed. Evidence of some indigenous desire for an inclusive community organization, the short-term use of organizers, the public affirmation of the principles of self-determination, and the encouragement of controversy to develop internal group cohesiveness characterize IAF organizational strategy.

In the Woodlawn Organization's early days, the University of Chicago was a major enemy, and they became involved in a controversy over land clearance and acquisition proposals. The vigorous opposition to the organization by Harold Fey, then the managing editor of *The Christian Century*, and by Walter Kloetzli, then the Secretary for Urban Church Planning of the National Lutheran Council, further highlighted the controversy over the organization, its sponsorship, methods, and objectives.[1]

TWO, as the organization is called, has been politically militant. It has used mass demonstration techniques, protest marches at City Hall, and similar procedures to attempt to obtain redress of ills in Woodlawn. This chapter is not designed to evaluate The Woodlawn Organization's activities but is focused upon two issues related to the organization.

The first issue emerged because TWO is an organization of organizations. Since its constitutive members are other organizations rather than individual persons, some churches *qua* churches became constitutive members of The Woodlawn Organization. This phenomenon raised the question of the proper relationship between churches and such organizations.

The second issue emerged because of TWO's use of power, understood as the ability to attain one's own will in conflict with other wills, and its insistence upon loyalty to the organization. The theological interpretation of these issues here both affirms and rejects dimensions of The Woodlawn Organization's approach to the resolution of certain problems afflicting metropolitan areas in the United States.

This chapter is divided into two major sections. The first section describes alternative ways of conceptualizing the nature of voluntary associations; the final section develops a typology of community and service organizations and attempts to evaluate The Woodlawn Organization. The evaluation of TWO, based upon one of the options discussed below, is related to the discussion of The Woodlawn Organization in the first portion of the final section.

Alternative Interpretations of the
Nature of Voluntary Associations

The central thesis of this section is that many Protestant churches violate their historical-theological traditions when they become members of The Woodlawn Organization because membership as a church identifies the Christian faith too closely with particular political, social or economic causes and programs. They have responded to an organization and to a theory of organization which is informed by an alternative understanding of the nature of voluntary associations. Because the orga-nization probably has contributed to the quest for justice by reducing an imbalance of political power in the city of Chicago, the development of this thesis does not imply a rejection of TWO's program of political action; but it does challenge the manner in which some of the Protestant churches in Woodlawn have supported this organization.

The implications of alternative perspectives on the nature of reality for the understanding of the Church and its relation to community organiza-tions must be considered here, but the relation of voluntary associations to the political order, and the relation of the political order to other forms of human social organization are not explored systematically. Though some historical references and some questions of fact are introduced, the primary focus is upon the understandings of the nature of the Chruch and community organizations which arise from alternative world views.

Four or five broad perspectives on the nature of reality may be provi-sionally delineated. The number depends upon whether one differenti-ates the Good of Plato and the God of the Bible. As the elements which permit the typological formulation are actually inextricably interrelated, the types which are developed distort the actual situation to some extent. Even so, the types are useful heuristically to define alternative perspec-tives which are, at one level, provisionally discernible.

A broad division may be made between phenomenological and onto-logical perspectives on the nature of reality. In the former case, neither a world behind the world nor a reality behind appearance is posited. In the latter case, some reality behind or enmeshed in appearance or some "known" behind or enmeshed in experience is affirmed.

Two phenomenological options are possible. One may emphasize either the self-affirming character of men's actions or the forms and circumstances to which man's choices are related. For proponents of the former view, voluntary associations consist of any group of persons who decide to organize for whatever purposes they choose. Viewing any human situation as a power struggle, they evaluate and interpret volun-tary associations by the degree of power they exercise. They understand power as the ability to achieve one's own will in conflict with other wills. They grant no distinction in principle between various types of voluntary associations, for they reduce all of them to a common power denomina-tor.[2] Proponents of the latter view differentiate voluntary associations by the type of subject matter to which they relate and the goals they seek. Men may deliberately choose to join or to create voluntary associations related to specified objects and may develop goals or objectives for these associations.

These two phenomenological perspectives are of special interest here. The second perspective has traditionally informed Roman Catholic theory of social organization. Special interest organizations, defined by their subject matter and the situation, have been spawned from the supernatural parent organization, and a reflective relationship has been established between the Roman church and these groups. Various Catholic social action groups, for example, are informed by this perspective. The goals or objectives are developed by the Church, and the voluntary association engages in programs designed to attain the objectives.

The Woodlawn Organization has been explicitly informed by the former perspective but there is the possibility that it is informed implicitly by the latter. It is difficult to understand how the Catholic Church could permit such heavy direct involvement of its Woodlawn parishes in TWO unless it had some direction over TWO, for otherwise it would be an external voluntary association. This analysis is based only upon theoretical reflection about the nature of various types of voluntary associations; no empirical data are presented here. There is no reason why theory and practice must converge in this situation, for a wide range of empirical data indicate that profound changes are taking place in the Catholic Church in the United States. Practice may well have been changing before theory in Woodlawn.

Two broad ontological perspectives are also formally possible. One may emphasize underlying elements or components which determine human behavior or a transcendent dimension to which man should relate. Proponents of the first perspective reject the idea of a "voluntary" association. The social scientist's task is to discern the underlying causes which give rise to associations called "voluntary" or to develop "laws" of institutional behavior. No one participating directly in the Woodlawn controversy has entertained this perspective, so it may be dismissed here.

Protagonists of the second ontological perspective envision a world transcending the world. This transcendent or "depth" dimension gives one's life its meaning and illumines its destiny. They may emphasize either form, the rational side of experience involving relatively changeless principles and eternal concepts or forms of definiteness, or dynamics, the power or creative side of experience involving change and emergent novelty.

Those who emphasize form maintain that reason leads one to the vision or experience of the Good. They would distinguish voluntary associations which arise in response and bear witness to this transcendental vision from other associations formed for a variety of more special reasons. Although they would hold that the systematic and hierarchical ordering of the forms leads to an intrinsic interrelatedness of various types of human associations, they would provisionally distinguish the religious institution from other forms of human association.

Interpreters differ in their assessment of the static and dynamic dimensions in this Platonic perspective and of its relation to Christian perspectives. Those who emphasize the static dimensions of the Good contrast it with Protestant views of God, but those who emphasize the dynamic dimension of the Good compare it with Protestant views of God. In any case, proponents of the dynamic perspective stress the dynamic character of the Divine. Most Christian interpreters affirm God's Self-revelation in Jesus as the Christ who reveals His ultimate character as Redemptive Love. They locate the Church's uniqueness in its nature as an institution based upon the Divine initiative.

Christian interpreters who base the Church's uniqueness on God's initiative may disagree about the proper relation of the Church to humanly established voluntary associations such as community organizations. Protagonists may insist on an unqualified distinction between the Church and human voluntary associations, may relate the Church to human voluntary associations but still distinguish the Church from them, or may deny the need for a distinction between the Church and human voluntary associations. An examination of these three alternative views of the relation between the Church and other voluntary associations will help in discerning the implicit or explicit presuppositions of Christian interpreters who hold differing views of the proper relation between the Church and The Woodlawn Organization.

Two variations of the first option are possible. First, protagonists may affirm a radical distinction between the Church and other forms of human association. Although counseling the Christian to serve and participate in the world, they place all social institutional forms sharply under God's judgment. Protagonists reject on principle the notion of a Christian social organization. This perspective has been reflected historically in Lutheran social ethics. Second, Christian believers may attempt a radical withdrawal from the world and refuse to participate in the principalities and powers of a fallen and sinful world. Proponents extend the radical distinction between the Church and other voluntary associations to Christians and non-Christians in the world. Sectarian groups such as the Amish and the Mennonites reflect this withdrawing perspective.

Two broad variations of the second option of relations between the Church and other voluntary associations are possible. Protagonists who affirm the dominance of dynamics over form blur the "Christian" character of social action. The Christian attempts to transform the world to attain a modicum of the harmony of life with life encompassed in his experiential confrontation of God as Redemptive Love, but he maintains the distinction between the Church and other forms of human associations. The Christian works through a variety of other associations to pursue the quest for justice in the world. This perspective has been reflected historically in many Calvinist groups.

Protagonists who affirm the dominance of form over dynamics can develop a clearer view of the "Christian" character of social action to guide the believer's behavior because rational principles are more unequivocally related to the Good. The monarchical and hierarchical nature of the Roman Catholic Church, the Church's directive role in the state, and the integrative role of a common Catholic belief system all reflect this formal emphasis on rules, principles, and structures. The relation between the supernatural Roman Catholic Church and various types of voluntary associations of the natural or phenomenological types has already been noted.[3]

Catholicism's greater clarity about an ideal form of social organization and about proper rules and regulations of justice has led to greater direct involvement in the political order than has been the case for some forms of Protestantism. As observed earlier, this difference is due to the dominance of form over dynamics in Roman Catholicism and the dominance of dynamics over form in Protestantism. The distinction is a qualified one, but it is important. It is associated with the close relation of Protestantism to Platonism and of Roman Catholicism to Aristotelianism.

Two variations of the final option are possible. In both cases, protagonists deny the distinction between the Church and other human associations, either on principle or on a *de facto* basis. One interpretation is associated with various radical sectarian perspectives. Protagonists envision a radical transformation and sanctification of the world to establish the ultimate harmony of life with life in the world. Members of certain Woodlawn churches which too easily equate the cause of the Afro-American with the Kingdom of God reflect this viewpoint. This revolutionary sectarian view is the obverse of the radical world-withdrawing view noted earlier.

The other interpretation is associated with various conservative sectarian perspectives. As proponents identify a particular extant culture or form of social organization more or less unqualifiedly with the experience of the ultimate harmony of things revealed in the Christ, they are politically very conservative.

Although they would differ sharply about the shape of the programs to which Christians should give their allegiance, protagonists of the two perspectives just described are relatively sanguine about direct Church support of specific political and economic causes and some voluntary associations.

There is a tantalizing relation between withdrawing sectarian views and revolutionary sectarian views, for there is a short theological and psychological distance between them. There may be, similarly, a close relation between both Calvinism and Catholicism and conserving sectarian views; the existence of certain forms of family, economic, cultural, and political organization in a nation elicits conserving emphases in both Catholicism and Calvinism. These issues are more fully explicated in Part Four, especially Chapter XII.

Although the relation of this typology of church-world perspectives to the contingencies of history is somewhat ambiguous, both the Lutheran and Calvinistic traditions have usually maintained a distinction between the Church and other types of voluntary associations even though they have developed different interpretations of the relations between love, power, and justice to guide Church members as they participate *qua* citizens in other types of voluntary associations. Because of the Church's distinctive character, some Protestants may be apprehensive about a local church's decision to become a constituent member of any natural super-organization. The problem is accentuated when the super-organization to which the church belongs is committed, as TWO is, to militant political action in behalf of a vested interest group. Protagonists sanctioning church membership in a super-organization such as TWO either reflect the third type of church-voluntary association relation or maintain a radically situational social ethic.

Community Organizations and the Churches: An Interpretation

This section develops a typology of community or service organizations and agencies which is based on a phenomenological understanding of power. Power is understood here as the ability to attain one's will (individual or communal) in conflict with other wills. Because of finitude, ignorance and/or sin, transcendent ontological perspectives always incorporate this dimension of power in a more inclusive understanding. A typology based on this truncated understanding, therefore, is useful to a theologian who wants to develop an interpretation of the proper relation of Christian churches to contemporary community or service organizations and agencies in the United States.

Although an exhaustive typology of community or service organizations and agencies would include other dimensions, a three-fold typology based upon the organizations' relations to power structures and to political action is adequate for the purpose of this discussion. Some of the organizations within each type are confined to particular geographical areas; others are not.

The first type of community or service organizations and agencies includes associations which operate within the existing power structures, social-institutional organizations, and patterns of migration and social stratification in a metropolitan area. Although some may be latently disruptive, organizations and agencies of this type tend to support existing structures and patterns. They are minimally involved in direct political action. Such organizations are frequently criticized caustically by those who challenge and resist aspects of existing patterns. This negativism is as misplaced as an unqualified attack on organizations which challenge some of the existing structures and patterns of metropolitan areas in the United States.

Almost all agencies supported by broadly based welfare groups such as United Charities and the Community Fund are of this supportive type. Government social service agencies, most independent social agencies, settlement houses, the YMCA, the YWCA, the Boy Scouts, the Girl Scouts, and Parent-Teachers Associations are other examples of this type. In spite of well-known problems involving the differential use of these agencies and their services by people in various social strata, the element of direct service to persons in need incorporated in such supportive programs deserves the qualified approbation of all who are concerned with reducing human suffering and cultivating a more wholesome communal life.

The second type of community or service organizations and agencies includes associations which both challenge and affirm the existing power structures, social-institutional organizations, and patterns of migration and social stratification in a specific metropolitan area. Organizations and agencies of this type are directly included in the pressures and counterpressures of the political processes of metropolitan areas in the United States.

Neighborhood "improvement" organizations, which have usually resisted the influx of Afro-Americans into their residential areas, and organizations such as The Woodlawn Organization, which have employed political pressure to try to obtain specified objectives in their communities, illustrate alternative sub-types of this major type. Though these groups are neither revolutionary nor reactionary, they bend in one direction or the other. One sub-type, of which TWO is a prototype, seeks to transform the existing patterns; the other sub-type, of which white neighborhood improvements associations are prototypes, seeks to preserve existing patterns.

Some community or service organizations and agencies of this second type focus primarily not on a geographical community, but rather on special interests or special spheres of the social order. Special interest voluntary associations such as labor unions, better government groups, the A.C.L.U., and independent voter groups illustrate this type of association.

The final type of community or service organizations and agencies includes associations which envision a radical overthrow of existing power structures, social-institutional organizations, and patterns of migration and social stratification in a metropolitan area. Such organizations are not numerous in contemporary American metropolitan areas, but there are a few. The American Nazi Party, the John Birch Society, the Students for a Democratic Society, and some "civil rights" organizations radically reject existing forms of social organization. The groups cited illustrate two sub-types of extremism: one reactionary, the other revolutionary.

Although the general tendencies of an organization may permit it to be categorized as one of the three types, in actual practice no unequivocal case exists. Many supporting agencies, for example, are engaged in transformative work which may ultimately have profound implications for the social structure and patterns of a metropolitan area. This typology, focused upon political orientation and involvement, is not intended to be exhaustive, but it is useful in discerning the political style of various community or service organizations and agencies.

Both the more strongly political organizations and the less strongly political supportive harmonizing agencies are necessary. The former reflect the disharmony symbolized by the idea of the Fall; the latter, the harmony symbolized by the idea of Redemption. Although the Church *qua* Church should avoid membership in and unqualified support of any temporal principality or power, laymen may legitimately support organizations and agencies of the first two types. Because the basic social, economic, cultural, and political structures of the United States should be sustained, laymen should be discouraged from involvements with associations of the third type on theological grounds.[4]

These formal considerations must be supplemented by an evaluation of TWO before a more substantial judgment about the relation of local churches and church members to such organizations can be made. The Woodlawn Organization, a prototype of the second type of voluntary association, is geographically based and seeks to transform existing patterns. Four facts should be noted.[5]

First, The Woodlawn Organization is a super-organization composed of other voluntary associations in the Woodlawn area. This type of organizational structure leads to conflicts and disagreements at two levels. Policy disagreements among members of each constitutive organization contribute to disharmony within each of the constitutive bodies, and conflict between the various participating voluntary associations is always a possibility.

Second, TWO places a strong emphasis upon "loyalty" to minimize internal conflicts and to increase the probability of obtaining its political objectives. Third, the organization tends to oversimplify issues and to develop "enemies" of various kinds. The former phenomenon is characteristic of almost all politically motivated groups, while the latter is both a by-product of the former and a device to enhance group loyalty.

Finally, The Woodlawn Organization is committed to overt political action to obtain such things as better schools, more police protection, and better housing through self-determination in matters pertaining to the community. This activity creates conflicts with many established community or service organizations and agencies, but it does get some results. One may speculate, however, about the probable consequences if a large number of similar organizations developed to compete for a limited amount of governmental resources. Fortunately, these resources may be increased, for political pressure, within limits, may help produce greater resources as well as alternative allocations of existing resources.

Persons or organizations engaged in this type of parapolitical activity almost always underrate the supportive and coordinating effects of the established political order in the life of the community. They ignore or interpret positively the way in which direct and militant political activity disrupts the complex efforts of municipal government to provide services —welfare, police, fire and educational—for the entire city.

Certain dangers inhere in TWO's efforts to mold an instrument of political power. Supporters and critics of the organization and others similar to it should be sensitive to them. First, there is always the possibility that latent racial disharmony may manifest itself in riots because of the organization's militant activity.

Second, in the press toward order (the effort to achieve a stabilized community) and participation (the encouragement of loyalty to the organization), there is the danger of losing freedom (in the formal sense of self-choice) and individuality. In light of the disorganized nature of the Woodlawn area, these considerations are probably not too significant at the present time, but a corollary is the danger of idolatry implicit in the strong emphasis upon loyalty to the organization. This danger is related to TWO's lack of explicit informing principles other than self-determination and the development of "power" to force others to assent to TWO's demands.

Third, TWO's relations to the major political parties is complex because the organization is attempting to develop an independent center of political power in Woodlawn. The potentially anarchical character of such a movement should be carefully and continuously scrutinized. Attention should also be continually directed toward the bureaucratization of the organization. Its key professional leaders, because of their political power, will be subject to pressures and temptations as the major political parties and special interest groups try to gain their support. If the organization is successful in exercising "self-determination," its leaders will be targets for various people seeking their favor through legal and extra-legal means.

Finally, the character of the organization makes it vulnerable to manipulation by vested interest groups. TWO's loose structure and the importance of a small leadership group would permit either the leaders or a behind-the-scenes group to influence policy unduly. Such a development would, of course, be contrary to the avowed principle of "self-determination."

These considerations lead to an evaluation of The Woodlawn Organization and the churches' proper relation to TWO and similar organizations. TWO should be both supported and criticized. Insofar as the organization reduces the imbalance of political power in the metropolitan area and increases citizen participation in areas of low socio-economic status, TWO should be supported. As long as laymen in Woodlawn churches temper their support with proper reserve, they might well participate in TWO through their membership in other voluntary associations.

Both the structure of the organization and the emphasis on loyalty to the organization make continual internal criticism of TWO difficult, so every effort should be made to encourage continued discussions about its aims at all levels. Although religious professionals who encourage such reflection may find themselves under some pressure because of the division it may create, the leaders of the churches are in an especially strategic position for exercising this function. The propensity toward idolatry inherent in the press for organizational loyalty must be challenged, for persons informed by Christian perspectives must continually resist the efforts of any organization to obtain uncritical loyalty.

The churches might well offer a context in which the leaders, both lay and clergy, could explore the complexity of the social, economic, and political issues confronting the area. As an illustration of this complexity, there are many legitimate values other than those to which TWO is committed. In spite of the validity of some of the Woodlawn residents' protests against unfair differential treatment, resources are also needed for government social services in other community areas. Some degree of social differentiation in a major metropolitan area is inevitable. The realization of a mixed social status community area which some TWO members have proposed is problematic, but it is conceivable that in the short run such an objective might be obtained by direct government action. The longer term consequences of such action, even if it were politically possible, might be undesirable for the tension between the principles of equality appropriate to form and self-determination informed by excellence limit government intervention and necessitate some social differentiation in any community. Key leadership groups in TWO should be conscious of such problems and complexities; the churches are in a strategic position to foster such understanding.

The Christian faith contains an understanding of redemption which is not accentuated by The Woodlawn Organization because it emphasizes conflict. The coordinating and harmonizing role of government must have higher priority than any of the special interest groups which appeal to it. Although some TWO criticisms of welfare practices are undoubtedly justified, public and private social service agencies in the area warrant some support.

Although social-institutional structures support the quest for justice, it must be remembered that the Church's efforts to attain wholesome community life are centered in worship, education, and the support of harmonious interpersonal relations. Any church which minimizes this center of its life does so at its peril, for these components give the Church its distinctive reason for existence.

The Church *qua* Church should avoid direct membership in TWO or any other organization which participates directly in the claims and counterclaims of history. Its distinctive character is compromised when it becomes a direct participant in the political arena. Although the clergymen's special role in the churches should place some restraint on them, no categorical statement can or should be made about their participation in TWO through other groups of which they may be members. The laity can work most vigorously in TWO as citizens participating in the political process.

Some Protestant denominations have used benevolence funds to support community organizations like TWO. The use of such funds for these purposes without the explicit approval of the donors is suspect. Persons whose monies are supporting such programs should have the right to make a judgment about this use of their benevolences. Special offerings to support community organizations might be taken in the churches, but this decision should not be left to members of the ecclesiastical bureaucracy.

There are various ways to foster the quest for justice in the United States. Although the development of parapolitical community organizations constitutes one approach, others might well be more fruitful. In any event, church sponsorship of political and economic activities must be subject to the closest scrutiny because of the ambiguity of love-justice relations.[6]

Some proponents of TWO may find these judgments too negative. However, they should not be construed as a rejection of The Woodlawn Organization and its objectives. On the contrary, TWO should be supported, but with qualifications. The socio-economic conditions in Woodlawn need to be improved, and TWO is certainly committed to efforts to improve them.

PART THREE

Three Philosophical Sociologists:
Analyses and Critiques

Chapter VI

Emile Durkheim's Ordering of the Sciences: A Resume and a Critique

Emile Durkheim, Max Weber, and Talcott Parsons, three social theorists whose influence on the social scientific study of religion has been pervasive, are considered in Part Three. Since all three men are theorists of the highest rank, the fundamental issues which they raise are inevitably philosophical and theological. Attention is focused upon these issues here. Although Weber is relatively more open then Durkheim or Parsons, none of them ascribes a *sui generis* character to religious experience.

Each chapter in Part Three is divided into five sections. An introductory section is followed by a discussion of the theorist's ordering of the sciences. The theorist's understanding of the nature of religious experience is considered in the third section; the fundamental notions guiding the theorist's systematic understanding are delineated in the fourth section. The final section subjects the social theorist to an external critique informed by the philosophic perpsective of Alfred North Whitehead and Charles Hartshorne.

The analyses are focused upon the theorists' systematic writings for these works most adequately illumine their fundamental presuppositions. The discussions in Part Three do not deal adequately with the theorists' substantive findings. Knowledge of the theorists is presupposed here, but the reader who has not examined their writings extensively may still find the discussions evocative because the issues considered are general ones. Interpreters of the three figures who disagree with the analyses developed here may, for the same reason, find the discussions suggestive.

Three works are used to illumine the fundamental structure of Durkheim's theoretical understanding. The emphasis is on Durkheim's major work in the sociology of religion, *The Elementary Forms of the Religious Life*. At appropriate points, supplementary material from *Sociology and Philosophy* and *The Rules of Sociological Method* is introduced.[1]

It would be difficult to overestimate Emile Durkheim's influence on contemporary sociology. Much of the contemporary work in the sociology of religion in the United States, especially structural-functional analyses, is directly or indirectly informed by his theoretical perspective.

The Ordering of the Sciences in Emile Durkheim

Durkheim posits a multiplicity of the sciences and orders them in a relational manner as he moves from the most simple to the most complex subject matter. The elements or compounds which characterize the subject matter of a particular science are synthesized when they interact with each other to produce a new compound. This new compound is related to the elements or compounds which underlie it, but it is differentiable from them.

In "Individual and Collective Representations," Durkheim indicates that the distinction between psychology and sociology is based upon a difference between individual and collective representations.[2] In that essay, written in 1898, Durkheim suggests a hierarchy of inorganic, organic, mental and social spheres. As the different sciences are based on the different subject matter in each sphere, Durkheim posits four broad types of science—physical, biological, psychological and sociological.

One begins with the interaction of material bodies, the subject matter of mechanics and physics. These bodies may combine in different ways to produce compounds which are the subject matter of chemistry. Certain combinations of chemical compounds may lead to the emergence of organic life, the subject matter of biology. Interaction among these compounds may induce the emergence of individual mental life, which is the subject matter of psychology. Finally, the interaction of men occasions the emergence of collective ideas, which have their locus in that empirical reality which Durkheim terms "society." Sociology, the science which studies this subject matter, is at the apex of the hierarchy of the sciences because mental and physical life are at a maximum here. This classification may be termed an emergent horizontal hierarchy, a term coined to emphasize the phenomenological character of Durkheim's analysis.

Durkheim appeals to empirical observation to establish these differentiations because these differing objects impinge upon the observer:

Since observation has revealed the existence of an order of phenomena called representations, distinguishable by certain characteristics from all other natural phenomena, it is scarcely methodical to treat them as though they did not exist. Undoubtedly they are caused, but they are in their turn causes.[3]

This appeal to "certain characteristics" distinguishing representations from all other natural phenomena is typical of Durkheim and reminiscent of the Cartesian distinctions between primary and secondary qualities. This issue will be explored later when the fundamental notions in Durkheim's thought are considered.

The view developed in "Individual and Collective Representations" is reaffirmed in Durkheim's last and greatest major work, *The Elementary Forms of the Religious Life*.[4] As this analysis is concerned primarily with Durkheim's most mature and systematic formulations, this continuity is significant.

Durkheim concludes his discussion of the social origins of religion in *The Elementary Forms of the Religious Life* with a statement contrasting his understanding with scientific materialism. This passage sharply delineates Durkheim's grounds for the ordering of the sciences:

Therefore it is necessary to avoid seeing in this theory of religion a simple restatement of historical materialism: that would be misunderstanding our thought to an extreme degree. In showing that religion is something essentially social, we do not mean to say that it confines itself to translating into another language the material forms of society and its immediate vital necessities. It is true that we take it as evident that social life depends upon its material foundation and bears its mark, just as the mental life of an individual depends upon his nervous system and in fact his whole organism. But collective consciousness is something more than a mere epiphenomenon of its morphological basis, just as individual consciousness is something more than a simple efflorescence of the nervous system. In order that the former may appear, a synthesis *sui generis* of particular consciousnesses is required. Now this synthesis has the effect of disengaging a whole world of sentiments, ideas and images which, once born, obey laws all their own. They attract each other, repel each other, unite, divide themselves, and multiply, though these combinations are not commanded and necessitated by the condition of the underlying reality. The life thus brought into being even enjoys so great an independence that it sometimes indulges in manifestations with no purpose or utility of any sort, for the mere pleasure of affirming itself. We have shown that this is often precisely the case with ritual activity and mythological thought.[5]

Durkheim makes two important methodological affirmations in this passage. First, he relates religion to the material forms in society which are the underlying social structures, but he also ascribes an autonomy to the emergent phenomenon. Second, his references to attraction, division, multiplication, and repulsion suggest that a whole at each emergent level is composed of analytically separable parts.

Although any explanation necessitates a consideration of the parts because they are required to explain the origin of a phenomenon, the peculiar character of each level cannot be explained on the basis of the combination of the parts which have given rise to it. The scientist will try to discover the laws by which the parts on a given level combine to produce new parts or a new whole on the same level.

Durkheim, for example, decided to study the most primitive religion known in order to illumine the nature of all religion. He based this decision on the assumption that common underlying structural components exist which permit universal comparisons. These common structural components also allow Durkheim to develop an elaborate social morphology and to compare and contrast societies at various stages of social development.[6] They also introduce the possibility that some experiences are epiphenomenal.

Durkheim leaves himself in an ambiguous position. He hopes that the science of sociology will mature sufficiently to permit the development of laws to explain social phenomena and to predict their future configuration, but he also affirms the relative independence of the sciences. As just noted, Durkheim envisions that the objects of "higher" sciences emerge in the interaction and synthesis of objects of the "lower" sciences. Individual representations or ideas emerge out of the organic substructure of the human organism, and collective representations emerge out of the interaction of individual representations in groups.

Durkheim's desire to develop "laws" which govern the emergence of new configurations of collective representations presents him with a dilemma. Either the conditioning influence of the underlying substrata must cease, or else adequate knowledge of the laws of the lower strata will permit him to predict the character of the emergent phenomena.[7] Durkheim could resolve this dilemma in two ways without altering his understanding of the goals of sociological analysis. He may envision an ultimate unity of the sciences, or he may suggest the radical autonomy of each emergent level.

If he were to envision an ultimate unity of the sciences, Durkheim could begin either with the lowest stratum, material bodies, or with the highest stratum, collective representations. On the basis of an adequate understanding of the laws of either the lowest or the highest stratum, he could understand the laws governing any of the remaining strata. If he were to envision the radical autonomy of each "emergent" level, Durkheim could develop the laws of the phenomena of a given level independent of findings about phenomena in the other strata. Either of these alternatives would require a revision of the relations which he envisions between the various strata.

Moral philosophy and theology have no special subject matter for Durkheim, so they are residual disciplines which will be superseded by scientific sociological analysis.[8] In a lecture delivered about the time of the publication of *The Elementary Forms of the Religious Life,* Durkheim clearly stated his position:

> To this question [beyond the real where can the material for a satisfactory explanation of the fact that value is attributed to the ideal be found?] the theological hypothesis makes a sort of answer. It postulates the existence of the world of ideals as a supra-experimental, but none the less objective, reality from which our empirical reality derives and depends. Thus we are joined to the ideal as the source of our being. Quite apart from other difficulties raised by this explanation, once the ideal has been hypostatized in this way it has at the same time become immobile, and all means of explaining its infinite variability are lost to us. We know today that not only is the ideal different in different groups, but also that it *should* vary. The ideal of the Romans was not, and cannot be, ours, and the scale of values varies accordingly. These changes are not due to human blindness but are based in the nature of the facts. How may they be explained if the ideal is one unassailable reality? We should be forced to admit that the Divinity varies in space and in time, and how can this be explained? The changing condition of God could only be intelligible if He had to realize an ideal beyond Himself, and anyhow this merely shifts the problem but does not change it.
>
> By what reasoning can the ideal be said to be beyond nature and science? It manifests itself in nature and surely, then, depends upon natural causes. In order that it may be more than a mere possibility for speculation it must be desired, and must therefore have a force

capable of swaying our wills. Our wills alone can make it a living reality. Since this force must ultimately be translated in terms of muscular movement it cannot differ essentially from the other forces of the universe. Why should it not be possible to analyze it, to resolve it into its elements and find those causes that determine the synthesis from which it results.[9]

In the last part of this passage, Durkheim appeals to the observable physical effects of the ideal. He suggests that the ideal is a synthesis which should be explained by analyzing the parts from which it came. This suggested procedure coheres with Durkheim's understanding of the scientific method, for the development of knowledge in all the sciences is guided by the common methodological canon that knowledge accrues through the systematic observation of the effects of various "objects" upon other objects.

Durkheim does not systematically review the procedures used in studying various subject matters, but he does deal at great length with the objects which comprise the subject matter of sociology. These objects, "social facts," are provisionally discerned by the scientist through their universal presence in society and through the constraints they impose upon men. The object of sociological investigation is isolated by a preliminary definition based upon these external characteristics. Extended analysis may lead from these external characteristics to the internal characteristics of the object under study. As observed earlier, this "external-internal" contrast is comparable to the Cartesian distinction between "secondary" and "primary" qualities of an entity.

Durkheim's method of sociological analysis involves breaking a whole into its constituent parts. The comparative examination of various societies based upon the type and the degree of differentiation of crucial structural components which Durkheim develops in *The Rules of Sociological Method* presupposes the autonomy of the parts of a whole. This presupposition is also Cartesian.

As he has rejected traditional philosophy and theology, Durkheim attempts to resolve the classical philosophic problems which center upon the interpretation of concepts and of the categories—space, time, cause and motion—by ascribing their locus to society. His turn from nature to society to explain philosophic categories may be characterized as an objectivist phenomenological resolution of the issues under consideration. Durkheim summarizes his understanding of society:

. . . we must say that society is not at all the illogical or a-logical, incoherent and fantastic being which it has too often been considered. Quite on the contrary, the collective consciousness is the highest form of psychic life, since it is the consciousness of the consciousnesses. Being placed outside of and above individual and local contingencies, it sees things only in their permanent and essential aspects, which it crystallizes into communicable ideas.[10]

The character of the movement from nature to society is reminiscent of Plato's movement from becoming to being. Because society emerged from individuals, it possesses contingent dimensions, but the remains of its origins are progressively eliminated as it moves toward increasing universality and objectivity. Durkheim describes the process in this passage:

At the same time that it [society] sees from above, it sees farther; at every moment of time, it embraces all known reality; that is why it alone can furnish the mind with the moulds which are applicable to the totality of things and which make it possible to think of them. It does not create these moulds artificially; it finds them within itself; it does nothing but become conscious of them. They translate the ways of being which are found in all the stages of reality but which appear in their full clarity only at the summit, because the extreme complexity of psychic life which passes there necessitates a greater development of consciousness. Attributing social origins to logical thought is not debasing it or diminishing its value or reducing it to nothing more than a system of artificial combinations; on the contrary, it is relating it to a cause which implies it naturally. But this is not saying that the ideas elaborated in this way are at once adequate for their object. If society is something universal in relation to the individual, it is none the less an individuality itself, which has its own personal physiognomy and its idiosyncrasies; it is a particular subject and consequently particularizes whatever it thinks of. Therefore collective representations also contain subjective elements, and these must be progressively rooted out, if we are to approach reality more closely. But howsoever crude these may have been at the beginning, the fact remains that with them the germ of a new mentality was given, to which the individual could never have raised himself by his own efforts: by them the way was open to a stable, impersonal and organized thought which then had nothing to do except to develop its nature.

Also, the causes which have determined this development do not seem to be specifically different from those which gave it its initial impulse. If logical thought tends to rid itself more and more of the subjective and personal elements which it still retains from its origin, it is not because extra-social factors have intervened; it is much rather because a social life of a new sort is developing. It is this international life which has already resulted in universalizing religious beliefs. As it extends, the collective horizon enlarges; the society ceases to appear as the only whole, to become a part of a much vaster one, with indetermined frontiers, which is susceptible of advancing indefinitely. Consequently things can no longer be contained in the social moulds according to which they were primitively classified; they must be organized according to principles which are their own, so logical organization differentiates itself from the social organization and becomes autonomous. Really and truly human thought is not a primitive fact; it is the product of history; it is the ideal limit toward which we are constantly approaching, but which in all probability we shall never succeed in reaching.[11]

The social basis of consciousness permits Durkheim to attribute an evolutionary character to human thought and to religious ideas. The differentiation of thought forms from the social organizations which created them illumines the process of the progressive universalization of social consciousness. Just as individual consciousness achieves relative autonomy from its biological substratum, so collective consciousness achieves relative autonomy from individual consciousness and undergoes an inner development of its own.[12]

As has been noted, there is no *sui generis* object of religious devotion for Durkehim. Religion involves an interplay between collective representations and social structures. The following section traces this interplay in detail.

Durkheim's Treatment of Religion

Society is the underlying cause of religion for Durkheim. *The Elementary Forms of the Religious Life* traces the manner in which underlying social structures effect the emergence of religion. Because there is a single fundamental cause of religion, the study of the development of religion among Australian aborigines is a crucial experiment. The findings may be generalized to explain the origin of religion wherever it may occur, for it is due to the same social causes everywhere. Religion begins with the cult through which faith is created and recreated periodically.

Because of his interest in the relation between underlying social structures and emergent collective representations, this concern with origins is a persistent feature of Durkheim's work. There is a shift in emphasis and interest in his later works, but it is doubtful if this shift represents a change in Durkheim's basic understanding. An increased interest in "collective representations," which is suggested by the 1898 paper cited earlier, is evident in his later writings.

This interest in origins persisted, however, for a large portion of *The Elementary Forms of the Religious Life* is devoted to the origins of religion. At the same time, the last part of that work discusses the development of collective representations. The fluid and dynamic character of these emergent collective representations is evident in this treatment. *The Elementary Forms of the Religious Life* is the only major empirical investigation that Durkheim wrote after he developed fully the idea that collective representations have considerable autonomy. The fluidity of collective representations may illumine Durkheim's observation that science is perennially incomplete, for science is based on collective representations purged of subjective elements. Durkheim's views are inherently ambiguous, because he both relates collective representations to underlying social structures and ascribes a relative autonomy to the emergent representations.

The first portion of *The Elementary Forms of the Religious Life* follows the procedure for scientific investigation outlined in *The Rules of Sociological Method.* Because all social facts may be identified by the force and constraint they display, Durkheim isolates the components of religious phenomena displaying such characteristics. This delineation leads to the famous definition of religion which permits him to identify the phenomenon in order to study it futher:

> *A religion is a unified system of beliefs and practices relative to sacred things, that is to say, things set apart and forbidden—beliefs and practices which unite into one single moral community called a Church, all those who adhere to them.* [13]

The basic commonality of religious phenomena in all epochs and in all cultures permits Durkheim to make this relatively inclusive definition of a church. Having identified the subject of his investigation, Durkheim proceeds to examine the causes of religious phenomena.

All religions sublimate and idealize both the good and evil components of society. The ideal, the natural product of social life, is formed during the intensive psychic and social interaction associated with times of crisis. Durkheim acknowledges that the collective ideals are individualized in men, for each person understands them in his own fashion and gives them a special emphasis. He maintains, however, that to understand this individuation it is sufficient "... to connect it with the social conditions upon which it depends."[14]

Religion does not possess a special cognitive quality, for the "objectivity" of society is something which the scientist can observe by discerning the force and constraint it exercises upon its members. This "objectivity" of society permits the scientist to explain on a natural basis that which has previously been explained supernaturally. The proper conception of the locus of religious beliefs will enable the scientist to understand the conflict between religion and science and to predict the future development of the relations between them.

Because religion lacks this special cognitive quality, Durkheim feels that the speculative role assigned to religion in the past will regress. The regression of the speculative role does not mean, however, that religion will pass away, for the cult and the faith are eternal elements in religion. The conflict between science and religion, as Durkheim conceives it, centers upon the speculative component of religion. Durkheim views the relation between the speculative function of religion and science as follows:

> ... Religion sets itself to translate these realities [nature, man, society] into an intelligible language which does not differ in nature from that employed by science; the attempt is made by both to connect things with each other, to establish internal relations between them, to classify them and to systematize them.[15]

Durkheim envisions a successive assimilation by science of this speculative function of religion:

> ... Men cannot celebrate ceremonies for which they see no reason, nor can they accept a faith which they in no way understand. To spread itself or merely to maintain itself, it must be justified, that is to say, a theory must be made of it. A theory of this sort must undoubtedly be founded upon the different sciences, from the moment when these exist; first of all, upon the social sciences, for religious faith has its origin in society; then upon psychology, for society is a synthesis of human consciousnesses; and finally upon the sciences of nature, for man and society are a part of the universe and can be abstracted from it only artificially.[16]

Science, which is concerned with the speculative side of religion, will not supplant faith which is an impetus to action. Although the future religion will inevitably move beyond science in action because science is always fragmentary and incomplete, the future religion must affirm science.

Durkheim gives the scientist a special and peculiar place of distinction in the social order. This view places Durkheim in the company of Democritus and Lucretius for they also held that the scientist possessed a special understanding of the nature of reality.

The common source of science, religion and morals in society resolves the alleged conflict between science and religion. Durkheim suggests an apparent contradiction between man's need to leave his individuality by raising himself to the control of impersonal laws and the obligation of impersonal law to incarnate itself in individuals, but he maintains that the contradiction can be overcome. Impersonal reason is merely a synonym for collective thought; therefore, the mutual relation between society and the individual resolves the apparent contradiction. Because social life involves both ideas and practices, the impersonality extends both to ideas and to behavior.

Durkheim ascribes characteristics to society which some theists ascribe to the Divine in the following passage:

> ... for society has a creative power which no other observable being can equal. In fact, all creation, if not a mystical operation which escapes science and knowledge, is the product of a synthesis. Now if the synthesis of particular conceptions which take place in each individual consciousness are already and of themselves productive of novelties, how much more efficacious these vast syntheses of complete consciousnesses which make society must be! A society is the most powerful combination of physical and moral forces of which nature offers us an example. Nowhere else is an equal richness of different materials, carried to such a degree of concentration, to be found. Then it is not surprising that a higher life disengages itself which, by reacting upon the elements of which it is the product, raises them to a higher plane of existence and transforms them.[17]

The "objective" character of society and nature, Durkheim submits, opens up the possibility of an alternative explanation of man's distinctive traits. They will no longer be put outside experience, but, rather, they will be explained by the superindividual reality which man experiences in society. A progressive "purging" of the subjective factor in collective representations offers the promise of moral progress in the future because higher moral laws are embodied in later collective representations. Science will play a major role in this "purging," for it will explain how society gives man his distinctive characteristics and will inform the faith which is a part of the religious phenomenon.

The Fundamental Informing Notions in Durkheim

The interaction of elements or components which combine in a synthesis to produce a new "object" is absolutely fundamental to Durkheim's ordering of the sciences. Insofar as a spatial image is useful, it might be suggested that Durkheim entertains an unfolding understanding of the sciences. He moves from the most simple subject matter, which embodies physical elements, to the most complex subject matter, which embodies reason.

His insistence that all of these objects are embedded in nature suggests a phenomenological assessment. Durkheim does not appeal to a world behind the world to explain experience; rather, he affirms a reflective relationship between a series of objects, all of which are on the phenomenological level.[18] It was suggested earlier that to emphasize its phenomenological nature Durkheim's ordering of the sciences might be termed an emergent horizontal hierarchy.

The horizontal hierarchy begins with material bodies, the subject matter of mechanics and physics, and progresses through objects of increasing complexity to collective representations which, together with social structures, make up the subject matter of sociology. In Durkheim's view "meaning" and "value" find their locus in society, for man participates in the society which is a part of him. Because of this participation in society and this internalization of values, man not only feels compelled to respond to certain values, but he also desires to respond to these values.

The objects of study in all the sciences are provisionally identified by the force they display, for the scientist can only discern these objects if they have some impact upon him or others. Science attempts to connect things with one another: to classify them, to systematize them and to establish internal relationships between them. Science perfects its method by purging all accidental elements. It brings a general spirit of criticism to all of its activities and surrounds itself with precautions to eliminate bias and all subjective influences.[19]

The scientist begins by making a preliminary identification of his object of study. On the basis of its external characteristics, he establishes a preliminary definition of the object of investigation. He makes further analyses to show the connection of things with each other and to establish internal relations. He does this by analyzing the components to which the object is related. He considers both a particular level of emergence and its relations to other levels.

Durkheim's procedure of scientific analysis implies a fairly complex knower-known relationship.[20] The object of study is discerned by the observer through some of its secondary qualities which relate the knower to the known. A comprehension of the factors contributing to the object of knowledge is gained through an appropriate method of scientific analysis.

Durkheim examines crucial "parts" to explain or to characterize a "whole." This whole-part relation is implicit in the knower-known relationship just described. Because he emphasizes common underlying material, biological, and social components, Durkheim makes cross-cultural comparisons between contemporary societies and between societies in different historical epochs. The relative autonomy of collective representations, however, prevents Durkheim from adopting a deterministic viewpoint. On his own terms, Durkheim is clearer about antecedent causes than about future possibilities.

A Critique

Durkheim develops a multiplicity of the sciences based upon different types of subject matter. The less complex sciences deal with physical objects; the more complex sciences, with objects in which mental aspects are dominant. In contrast to Durkheim's bifurcation of physical and mental objects, it is held here that both physical and mental factors are unified in the becoming of all actual entities.

The physical component is the objectification in an emerging actual entity of occasions in that entity's causal past as the entity begins to become what it is to be. This physical pole of an actual entity is "succeeded" by a mental pole which involves the appropriation of forms of definiteness embodied originally in God's primordial nature and mediated to the emerging entity by Him.[21] Every actual entity, then, is dipolar, and its process of becoming involves the unification of its physical and mental poles in a unique synthesis.

Differences emerge between the several empirical sciences because of differences in the relative importance of the physical and mental poles in the object under investigation. The massive dominance of the physical pole of experience in so-called inorganic objects, for example, leads them to reproduce their causal past in the present with a minimum of novelty. The much greater importance of the mental pole and of decision in human beings, in contrast, permits them to introduce far more novelty into the present as they become what they are.

A provisional multiplicity of the sciences based upon the relative importance of the two components in the object under investigation is suggested here. Yet, the sciences are also provisionally unified since all entities reflect the same fundamental categories; therefore, the differences between the several sciences are a difference of degree rather than of kind. This is so even though the difference of degree is so great that methods and objectives of investigation in the social studies differ greatly from methods and objectives of investigation in the sub-human sciences.

Durkheim assumes sharp distinctions between physical and material objects and that a whole may be analyzed by considering its component parts. In contrast, it is held here that these distinctions are equivocal and that a whole is more than the sum of its component parts. It follows that Durkheim's precision in explaining origins is excessive and the value of cross-cultural comparisons is less than Durkheim suggests.

Durkheim's approach is too mechanistic and too reductionistic. Although the generality of physical, mental and unifying dimensions in experience and the pervasiveness of certain structural forms in human societies make comparative efforts suggestive, the peculiar wholes which constitute various historical epochs and various societies make cross-cultural comparisons considerably more fuzzy than Durkheim indicates. This issue will be considered again in Chapter VIII because Talcott Parsons also presupposes the discreetness of the parts from which he constructs his system.

Durkheim's horizontal hierarchy of the sciences and his material-non-material distinction produce serious difficulties in his conception of society. Durkheim does attempt to deal with some realm beyond man, but his approach is inadequate. It completely begs the questions of the presence of a lure toward coherence or of a lure toward greater intensity of feeling prior to the emergence of society.

Durkheim suggests that "society," which is "conscious," is becoming less "personal" because the scars of its origins are being progressively purged. It is held here that exactly the opposite is happening to the Ultimate Receptor of all the creatures that have become. He is the Supreme Person because He alone can receive everlastingly all that the world offers. He is also the only fully conscious entity since consciousness is the contrast of what is not but might be with what is. Because the Divine encompasses all potentiality and all actuality, He can contrast supremely what is not but might be with what is.

Durkheim's view of emergent levels bears a tantalizing relation to process philosophy and to emergent evolution. As Durkheim's formulation stands, however, society is not able to do all that is required of a transcendent referent. The quasi-deification of society is inadequate, for it does not permit a coherent resolution of philosophic problems. An entity who in some sense is transcendent, omniciscient, omnipotent and omnipresent is necessary to resolve philosophic issues and to support an understanding which interprets religious experience in a *sui generis* way.

The phrase "in some sense" is included to emphasize the idea that the Divine is also immanent and finite. God transcends the world, but He is also immanent in the world because He contributes to the actualization of all creatures. He is omniscient in the sense that His primordial nature embodies the once-for-all envisagement of all potentiality, but He is not omniscient in the sense that He knows or includes the future, because the future is yet to become. He is omnipotent in the sense that He can respond sensitively to all that the world offers him, but He is not omnipotent in the sense that He can impose His will on creatures. Creatures contribute to the Divine Life, as they "decide" what they are to be. He is omnipresent in the sense that He contributes to the becoming of all creatures and retains perfectly and everlastingly all the creatures that have become, but not in the sense that He pervades all space because space itself becomes in the creatures. There is a becoming of continuity but not a continuity of becoming.

Durkheim's effort to place philosophy and theology in residual categories is unsatisfactory, for the issues with which they deal are perennial. They cannot be relegated into permanent impotence by Durkheim's understanding of the nature of science and society. The nature of philosophic categories, the emergence of novelty, and the problem of sense perception illustrate Durkheim's difficulties.

Although certain special formulations of the categories of space and time are associated with social organization as Durkheim suggests, the categories *qua* categories cannot be explained in Durkheim's empirical manner.

Durkheim does not handle creative thought coherently, for a thinker may probe a form which has never been apprehended before or an individual may experience a form which has never been realized before. Durkheim's "society" does not serve as the locus of such novelty.

Durkheim treats sense perception most inadequately, for he neither examines the basis upon which the human organism experiences his world nor explores many of the factors which must be considered to develop an adequate and coherent explanation of perception. He merely affirms that an object of scientific study is originally isolated by the force and constraint it manifests, but he does not discuss the way in which the relation between the object and the observer is established. Society, as Durkheim conceives it, is unable to mediate such an experience from an object to a subject.

Durkheim maintains a type of social relativism and displays some ambiguity about the relation between the individual and his social environment. Although he struggles with the question of norms, he is unwilling to suggest normative forms of human social organization which might be a lure to men. Because the interrelation of fact and value is fundamental in human experience, a social theorist should delineate ideal forms of social organization even though such forms may not be appropriate for a given society in a given historical epoch.

Although Durkheim does not ignore the individual, he displays a great deal of ambivalence about the individual's role. Durkheim minimizes the significance of the individual in *The Rules of Sociological Method.* His sharpest statement occurs in this famous footnote:

> Psychological phenomena can have only social consequences when they are so intimately united to social phenomena that the action of the psychological and of the social phenomena is necessarily fused. This is the case with certain sociopsychological facts. Thus, a public official is a social force, but he is at the same time an individual. As a result he can turn his social energy in a direction determined by his individual nature, and thereby he can have an influence on the constitution of society. Such is the case with statesmen and, more generally, with men of genius. The latter, even when they do not fill a social function, draw from the collective sentiments of which they are the object an authority which is also a social force, and which they can put, in a certain measure, at the service of personal ideas. But we see that these cases are due to individual accidents and, consequently, cannot affect the constitutive traits of the social species which, alone, is the object of science. The restriction on the principle enunciated above is not, then, of great importance for the sociologist.[22]

Durkheim treats inadequately the innovative and transcendent character of human decision. Human decisions do affect the shape of the social order and contribute to the future. Consideration of the acts of men is necessary to adequate social analysis.

Although Durkheim rejects the fact-value dichotomy which Kant posited and Weber affirmed, some variety of Platonism is more helpful in resolving the dichotomy. Durkheim holds that society is the locus of value; it is maintained here that values are located in God and in the subject-objects of experience. (The term "subject-object" is used to convey the notion that creatures are both subjects and objects. As a creature becomes by unifying its physical and mental poles, it is an emerging subject. After it has become what it decides to be, it is an objective datum for other creatures.) Other subject-objects are appropriated by an emerging subject who may reshape them but who cannot completely eliminate them from his experience. A relativity of specific values is implied here, for the emerging subject-object must appropriate values from a given context. Durkheim is partially correct in locating value in society, but society should be expanded to include all subject-objects and should be related to an overarching lure for intensity of feeling and for harmony. Durkheim rejects this transcendental source of value.

The nature of the subject-object of religious devotion is inextricably related to the question of value and the Good. Durkheim ingeniously relates science and religion, but separating the rational component of religion from faith and a cult is unsatisfactory because reason, which is embodied in the primordial nature of God, participates in all that is. Although some contingent cognitive formulations are certainly separable from religion, Durkheim's attempted separation of reason itself from religion is impossible. Durkheim's reason which explains the cult and faith is reason which undercuts the *sui generis* character of religious experience, for the person who believes that society is the foundation of religious experience can scarcely affirm the *sui generis* nature of such experience.

Although religious experience has a social and a cultic dimension, it also has a solitary dimension: religious experience reflects man's response to and integration of the physical and conceptual phases of his experience. Man receives the data for religious experience from his world, so religion is social. Man harmonizes and integrates these data internally, so religion is also private. The two facets of religious experience are reciprocal, but both community and solitariness contribute to religious experience.

There is not as much self-centeredness or self-consciousness among primitive people as there is among some contemporary people, but Durkheim's view that primitive religion is essentially social is incorrect. Durkheim himself observes that some of the behavior of primitives which he terms "set aside" is personal. Because of his total theoretic perspective, he terms such behavior "magic."

As Durkheim suggests, the awareness of a dimension of sacredness, incorporating a "set apartness" or transcendence, is indispensable for genuine religious experience. The subject-object which gives rise to religious experience is, nevertheless, inextricably interrelated with the world. Durkheim's theoretic perspective leads him to contrast too sharply the sacred and the profane. God's functioning in the universe needs to be secularized, for God is at work in the world whether or not the creatures of the world are aware of His presence.

Although his method is basically one of construction and analysis, Durkheim's understanding of the scientific method is partially appropriate in special contexts. It was widely used in classical mechanics and in nineteenth-century physics and chemistry. In these fields, the method has since been challenged or supplemented by field theory and relativity perspectives. Durkheim's method is also inadequate in the social sciences. It minimizes the creative aspect of human life and focuses inordinate attention on man's causal past rather than upon his emergent possibilities. As observed earlier, the method is too mechanistic and reductionistic to deal adequately with many aspects of human life.

The rigid character of Durkheim's method prevents the voyage toward larger philosophic generalities. It precludes the development of metaphysics and undercuts the quest for truth, beauty, and goodness. All the sciences except metaphysics employ a method of difference. The scientist contrasts what is with what is not as he develops the laws appropriate to his subject matter. The method of difference collapses, however, when faced with the most general questions which consider the pervasive and all inclusive dimensions of experience. The propositions applicable to all conceivable actual entities are properly termed metaphysical; those which apply to the Supreme Entity, theological. Metaphysical and theological analyses should supplement and inform analyses made by all other sciences. The pervasive lure for truth, beauty, and goodness means that such supplementation is vital to the study of man. As a meaning-seeking, meaning-positing entity, man must explore alternative modes of thought and satisfy the desire for truth, beauty, goodness, hope, peace, and adventure beyond the provinces of particular sciences.

Chapter VII

Max Weber's Ordering of the Sciences:
A Resume and a Critique

Max Weber's great analytic power and his widespread influence among contemporary social scientists make him an especially appropriate subject for consideration. The significant contrasts between Weber's method of ordering the sciences and the methods of Emile Durkheim and Talcott Parsons further commend him.

Weber's emphasis upon human acts of will parallels the understanding of many Protestant theologians. His perspective is more readily appropriated by them than the perspectives of either Durkheim or Parsons. Although common historical roots never adequately explain common thought patterns, one might note that the neo-Kantian tradition informing Weber's theoretic views is common among Protestant theologians, especially German ones.

This analysis is focused on portions of the published texts of two speeches, "Politics as a Vocation" and "Science as a Vocation," which Weber delivered at Munich University in 1918.[1] The issues of special interest here are clearly illumined in these two essays, which are among Weber's last writings. Supplementary materials from *The Theory of Social and Economic Organization* are introduced where necessary for clarification.[2]

Weber's Ordering of the Sciences

Weber makes a fundamental division between the natural sciences and the social sciences because the objects of investigation are different. Man is a meaning-seeking, meaning-positing animal capable of exercising his will and manifesting his power in confrontation with other wills. Due to these characteristics of man, the social sciences have to deal with human decisions and the interaction between value orientations and social-institutional configurations, while the natural sciences focus either upon non-human phenomena or upon the sub-human part of man. Neither the natural nor the social sciences answer the question of life's meaning or purpose. This question is answered by man who wills or chooses a meaning or purpose.

Weber makes a neo-Kantian distinction in "Science as a Vocation" when he suggests that scientific work presupposes the validity of the rules of logic and of scientific method. The peculiarly human problem in scientific work is the meaning which it allegedly yields.

Weber begins his discussion of the ordering of the sciences in "Science as a Vocation" with a consideration of the sciences most remote from man's will, his decision-making center. He moves toward those sciences which involve man's shaping, deciding, and creating activities and closes with a discussion of types of ethics. As the decision to act is at the very center of man's will, the science of ethics is the "last" science. Weber emphasizes the necessity for man to make decisions, but he does not prescribe the kind of decision which should be made. This carefully ordered lecture provides the basis for this interpretation of Weber's ordering of the sciences, but it will be supplemented by relevant passages from *The Theory of Social and Economic Organization.*

In "Science as a Vocation" Weber develops a broad six-fold grouping of the sciences. He refers first to the physical sciences and cites physics, chemistry and astronomy as examples. The intent of such sciences is ". . . to know the ultimate laws of cosmic events as far as science can construe them."[3] Weber next mentions medicine, which he considers a natural science. Although he does not explicitly cite biology or psychology, his reference to medicine suggests that biology and psychology are also natural sciences.

It is revealing that Weber never dealt extensively with psychology. This alleged lacuna, mentioned by many critics, should be interpreted in the light of Weber's neo-Kantian philosophic orientation. Insofar as psychology examines biological and physiological aspects of man, it is a natural science. However, if an analyst focuses on subjective meanings and the rational consideration of alternative courses of action, he is dealing with a sociological problem. The following passage supports this interpretation:

. . . [it is erroneous] to regard any kind of 'psychology' as the ultimate foundation of the sociological interpretation of action. The term 'psychology,' to be sure, is to-day understood in a wide variety of senses. For certain quite specific methodological purposes the type of treatment which attempts to follow the procedures of the natural sciences employs a distinction between 'physical' and 'psychic' phenomena which is entirely foreign to the disciplines concerned with human action, at least in the present sense. The results of a type of psychological investigation which employs the methods of the natural sciences in any one of various possible ways may naturally, like the results of any other science, have, in specific contexts, outstanding significance for sociological problems; indeed this has often happened. But this use of the results of psychology is something quite different from the investigation of human behaviour in terms of its subjective meaning. Hence sociology has no closer logical relationship on a general analytical level to this type of psychology than to any other science. The source of error lies in the concept of the 'psychic.' It is held that everything which is not physical is *ipso facto* psychic, but that the *meaning* of a train of mathematical reasoning which a person carries out is not in the relevant sense 'psychic.' Similarly the rational deliberation of an actor as to whether the results of a given proposed course of action will or will not promote certain specific interests, and the corresponding decision, do not become one bit more understandable by taking 'psychological' considerations into account. But it is precisely on the basis of such rational assumptions that most of the laws of sociology, including those of economics, are built up. On the other hand, in explaining the irrationalities of action sociologically, that form of psychology which employs the method of subjective understanding undoubtedly can make decisively important contributions. But this does not alter the fundamental methodological situation.[4]

Two observations should be made about this passage. First, sociological analysis should contrast a rational analytical model with an actor's actual course of action. Second, meaning and decision have central significance in sociological study. Psychology, which is concerned with subjective meanings, may prove useful to sociology, but sociology examines the implications of these meanings for the social order with the aid of a rationally developed interpretive framework.

The other groups of sciences which Weber enumerates in "Science as a Vocation" are all specifically human, for they involve men's works, actions and decisions. Aesthetics studies works of art which reflect human meaning because they are produced by men. This science, according to Weber, attempts to discern under what cultural conditions certain works of art are produced.

The science of jurisprudence establishes legal validity according to the rules of juristic thought. The rules consist partly of logically compelling forms and partly of the conventions which are part of a living community. Weber ultimately appeals to man's will to justify juridicial thought: man's acknowledgment that certain legal rules and certain methods of interpretation are binding makes them so. This legal positivism coheres with Weber's fact-value distinction and his emphasis on power.

The historical and cultural sciences make up Weber's fifth broad grouping. Their task is to understand and interpret the origins of political, artistic, literary and social phenomena. Although he does not include economic phenomena in this grouping, the omission is probably an oversight as Weber, in other contexts, places economics with the historical and cultural sciences. Historical consideration of origins both describes the work of men and the environment in which the work emerged.

The final clustering of disciplines includes sociology, history, economics, political science and those types of cultural philosophy which interpret these phenomena. The text suggests that the difference between the fifth and sixth groupings is one of emphasis and degree rather than of kind. The task of sociology, economics and political science is to analyze structures and positions. As this last grouping of sciences is of special interest here, Weber's treatment in "Science as a Vocation" will be supplemented extensively with material from *The Theory of Economic and Social Organization.*

> Most generally, sociology may be understood as that science which ... attempts the interpretive understanding of social action in order thereby to arrive at a causal explanation of its course and effects. In 'action' is included all human behaviour when and in so far as the acting individual attaches a subjective meaning to it. Action in this sense may be either overt or purely inward or subjective; it may consist of positive intervention in a situation, or of deliberately refraining from such intervention or passively acquiescing in the situation. Action is social in so far as, by virtue of the subjective meaning attached to it by the acting individual (or individuals), it takes account of the behaviour of others and is thereby oriented in its course.[5]

Sociology in this sense would include political science and economics as special sub-disciplines focused upon certain kinds of social action. Political science would study the processes of the distribution of power and attitudes toward power among groups within a state or between states. Economics would examine patterns and attitudes involved in the manufacture, distribution and acquisition of goods and services. Sociology may also be defined in a secondary sense as the study of honor or prestige. The style of life characteristic of various status groupings would be the focus of this limited type of study.

Weber's definition of sociology must be related to his definition of power. Power is "social action" in its exterior dimension. Weber defines power as "the probability that one actor within a social relationship will be in a position to carry out his own will despite resistance, regardless of the basis on which this probability rests."[6] "Will" power is manifest through status, class and party relations, so these relations are crucial in Weber's analyses. Status refers to the social order; it is distinguished by "style of life" and involves prestige and honor. Class refers to the economic order; it is distinguished by the production and distribution of goods and services and involves wealth. Party refers to the legal order; it is distinguished by rational manipulation of interests to attain one's own will and involves power *per se.* Parties may function in either the public or private sphere.

Weber's understanding of power in the political order is embodied in his definition of the modern state:

> . . . The primary formal characteristics of the modern state are as follows: It possesses an administrative and legal order subject to change by legislation, to which the organized corporate activity of the administrative staff, which is also regulated by legislation, is oriented. This system of order claims binding authority, not only over the members of the state, the citizens, most of whom have obtained membership by birth, but also to a very large extent, over all action taking place in the area of its jurisdiction. It is thus a compulsory association with a territorial basis. Furthermore, today, the use of force is regarded as legitimate only so far as it is either permitted by the state or prescribed by it. . . . The claim of the modern state to monopolize the use of force is as essential to it as its character of compulsory jurisdiction and of continuous organization.[7]

Rejecting efforts to define a state in terms of ends, Weber defines it in terms of his sophistic understanding of power. This interpretation of power is consistent with his distinction between statements of fact and of value. If states could be defined in terms of ends, a normative evaluation would be interjected into a "value-free" "scientific" definition of the state.

The emergence of the modern state is a consequence of the unification of various "wills." As competing men and groups attempted to attain power and exercise their own wills in opposition to other wills, power finally became centered in a single "will," the state. Weber does not hypostatize the state, for he constantly refers to the political leader who manifests his will in the state.

In the first part of "Politics as a Vocation," Weber traces this process of unification in several countries as various interest groups competed with one another. Different alliances in the several countries contributed to the different types of unified states which emerged from these conflicts of wills with wills. For example, Weber attributes great significance to the fact that in England the monarch made alliances with Parliament in opposition to an emerging civil service bureaucracy in opposition to the Reichstag. The former alliances fostered the development of democracy, and the latter alliances fostered the development of autocracy.

Political science traces this interplay of wills, relates them to subjective meanings, and sets them in the context of the political structures of a society. Weber's view gives political activity a dynamic character which defies the effort of political science to contain it by formal analysis even though tendencies and configuration may be discerned.

Weber's definition of economic action locates economics among the cultural sciences.

Action will be said to be 'economically oriented' so far as, according to its subjective meaning, it is concerned with the satisfaction of a desire for 'utilities' *(Nutzleistungen)*. 'Economic action' *(Wirtschaften)* is a peaceful use of the actor's control over resources, which is primarily economically oriented. Economically rational action is action which is rationally oriented, by deliberate planning, to economic ends. An 'economic system' *(Wirtschaft)* is an autocephalous system of economic action. An 'economic organization' *(Wirtschaftsbetrieb)* is a continuously organized system of economic action.[8]

Weber makes an important distinction between subjective and objective phenomena:

> The definition of economic action must be as general as possible and must bring out the fact that all 'economic' processes and objects are characterized as such entirely by the meaning they have for human action in such roles as ends, means, obstacles, and by-products. It is not, however, permissible to express this by saying, as is sometimes done, that economic action is a 'psychic' phenomenon. The production of goods, prices, or even the 'subjective valuation' of goods, if they are empirical processes, are far from being merely psychic phenomena. But underlying this misleading phrase is a correct insight. It is a fact that these phenomena have a peculiar type of subjective meaning. This alone defines the unity of the corresponding processes, and this alone makes them accessible to subjective interpretation.
> . . . The concept [of economic action] must take account, on the one hand, of the fact that utilities are actually sought after—including among them orientation to pecuniary acquisition for its own sake. But, on the other hand, it must also include the fact, which is true even of the most primitive self-sufficient economy, that attempts, however primitive and traditionally limited, are made to assure the satisfaction of such desires by some kind of activity.[9]

Weber incorporates two dimensions in his analysis. First, he insists that economic phenomena are more than mere psychic phenomena, for they are empirical processes subject to observation. Second, he notes that from the scientist's point of view economic phenomena do possess subjective meanings which must be considered.

Weber does not deny that economic action is related to "objective" needs, for economic action arises from man's physical necessities. However, because of man's ability to shape his world, the form which economic action takes and the economic system which evolves depend upon the subjective meaning which man gives as he responds to his basic physical needs. Discerning the meaning which men in a particular society ascribe to economic action is a necessary part of the economist's task.

In addition to sociology, economics and political science, Weber also includes history and cultural philosophy among the cultural sciences. If sociology is understood in the broad sense which Weber suggests, economics and political science will be sub-disciplines within this broader discipline. All social scientific analysis involves a consideration of social structures, human actions and subjective meanings, for social structures and processes are the result of the interplay between meanings, structures and human decisions.

Sociology, economics and political science deal with type concepts and generalized uniformities of empirical process; history deals with the individual and the discrete case. This distinction is extremely important, for the ultimate value of sociological analysis hinges on the relative importance of idiosyncratic cases compared with universal patterns. In his discussion of this matter, Weber states:

> It has continually been assumed as obvious that the science of sociology seeks to formulate type concepts and generalized uniformities of empirical process. This distinguishes it from history, which is oriented to the causal analysis and explanation of individual actions, structures, and personalities possessing cultural significance. The empirical material which underlies the concepts of sociology consists to a very large extent, though by no means exclusively, of the same concrete processes of action which are dealt with by historians. Among the various bases on which its concepts are formulated and its generalizations worked out, is an attempt to justify its important claim to be able to make a contribution to the causal explanation of some historically and culturally important phenomenon. As in the case of every generalizing science the abstract character of the concepts of sociology is responsible for the fact that, compared with actual historical reality, they are relatively lacking in fullness of concrete content. To compensate for this disadvantage, sociological analysis can offer a greater precision of concepts. This precision is obtained by striving for the highest possible degree of adequacy on the level of meaning in accordance with the definition of that concept. . . . It has already been repeatedly stressed that this aim can be realized in a particularly high degree in the case of concepts and generalizations which formulate rational processes. But sociological investigation attempts to include in its scope various irrational phenomena, as well as prophetic, mystic, and affectual modes of action, formulated in terms of theoretical concepts which are adequate on the level of meaning. In *all* cases, rational or irrational, sociological analysis both abstracts from reality and at the same time helps us to understand it, in that it shows with what degree of approximation a concrete historical phenomenon can be subsumed under one or more of these concepts. For example, the same historical phenomenon may be in one aspect 'feudal,' in another 'patrimonial,' in

another 'bureaucratic,' and in still another 'charismatic.' In order to give a precise meaning to these terms, it is necessary for the sociologist to formulate pure ideal types of the corresponding forms of action which in each case involve the highest possible degree of logical integration by virtue of their complete adequacy on the level of meaning. But precisely because this is true, it is probably seldom if ever that a real phenomenon can be found which corresponds exactly to one of these ideally constructed pure types. . . . Theoretical analysis in the field of sociology is possible only in terms of such pure types. . . .

It is important to realize that in the sociological field as elsewhere, averages, and hence average types, can be formulated with a relative degree of precision only where they are concerned with differences of degree in respect to action which remains qualitatively the same. Such cases do occur, but in the majority of cases of action important to history or sociology the motives which determine it are qualitatively heterogeneous. Then it is quite impossible to speak of an 'average' in the true sense. . . .

The theoretical concepts of sociology are ideal types not only from the objective point of view, but also in their application to subjective processes. In the great majority of cases actual action goes on in a state of inarticulate half-consciousness or actual unconsciousness of its subjective meaning.[10]

Weber emphasizes the abstract and theoretic character of sociology in this passage. As noted earlier, the usefulness of sociological analyses depends upon the value of this abstraction from historical processes. The perennial controversy between those historians who stress the uniqueness of historical configurations and those sociologists who emphasize the universality of structures and processes turns on their differing views of this whole-part question. If an historical epoch is more than the sum of the parts, sociological analysis using type concepts and seeking generalized uniformities of type processes will inevitably distort one's grasp of the epoch.

Weber attempts to resolve this issue by distinguishing between repeatable and non-repeatable ideal types. The repeatable ideal type refers to phenomena, such as the charismatic leader, which recur again and again; the non-repeatable ideal type, to phenomena, such as capitalism, which happen once because of a unique configuration of historical circumstances.

As the passage just quoted indicates, Weber uses "reason" in two ways. The sociologist uses "theoretic" reason to develop concepts which increase his understanding of the empirical situation under investigation. These concepts are constructs of theoretic reason and are not reflected precisely in any empirical social phenomenon. One of the things the sociologist studies through the use of theoretic reason is "technical" reason, reason focused on using the most efficient means to attain a given end. Technical reason is of great importance in the modern world, for the person who uses it or is subjectively aware of it believes that the processes which govern the world can be known and directed. The rationalization and "disenchantement" of the world to which Weber frequently refers is a consequence of the pervasive impact of technical reason in the modern world.

This discussion of reason leads to a consideration of Weber's view of the place of philosophy, ethics, and theology among the sciences. The related notions of "statement of fact," "statement of value," cultural philosophy, reason, and ethics occupy salient places in this consideration.

Philosophy is "critical." It examines the grounds upon which the sciences rest and demonstrates the futility of metaphysics or ontology developed with the aid of theoretic reason. Weber dismisses this approach to ontology in "Science as a Vocation." The proposition that science may be the ". . . 'way to true being,' the 'way to true art,' the 'way to true nature,' the 'way to true God,' and 'the way to true happiness' " is illusory.[11] Weber derives no meaning from the object of scientific investigation. This view, widespread in the neo-Kantian tradition of south Germany, presupposes a radical disjunction between the theoretic sciences and the practical sciences such as ethics and theology.

Weber is rigorously phenomenological. Theoretic reason, whether in the natural or the social sciences, is "value-free." It cannot lead one to "the good" or to an understanding of the "really real," for the object under investigation contributes nothing to the investigator. The object of study cannot lead one to value *qua* value or to an awareness or experience of the nature of ultimate reality.

Weber reflects this fundamental idea when he insists that the importance of subjective meaning is independent of the object toward which the meaning is directed. This viewpoint, for example, shapes his interpretation of Plato. In "Science as a Vocation" Weber asserts "Plato's passionate enthusiasm in *The Republic* must, in the last analysis, be explained by the fact that for the first time the *concept*, one of the great tools of all scientific knowledge, had been consciously discovered."[12] Weber does not base his assessment of *The Republic* upon an internal understanding of Plato's argument, for Plato would insist that his passionate enthusiasm in *The Republic* is a consequence of the fact that, through the appropriate use of dialectic and reason, he had penetrated to the Form of Forms, the Good, and had comprehended or experienced the relation between the forms—or concepts—and the Good. On Plato's own terms his comprehension is transrational, but not irrational.

Weber states his view of the disjunction between subjective meaning and the object of study clearly in the following passage from "Science as a Vocation."

> To take a practical political stand is one thing, and to analyze political structures and party positions is another. When speaking in a political meeting about democracy, one does not hide one's personal standpoint; indeed, to come out clearly and take a stand is one's damned duty. The words one uses in such a meeting are not means of scientific analysis but means of canvassing votes and winning over others. They are not plowshares to loosen the soil of contemplative thought; they are swords against the enemies: such words are weapons. It would be an outrage, however, to use words in this fashion in a lecture or in the lecture-room. If, for instance, 'democracy' is under discussion, one considers its various forms, analyzes them in the way they function, determines what results for the conditions of life the one form has as compared with the other. Then one confronts the forms of democracy with non-democratic forms of political order and endeavors to come to a position where the student may find the point from which, in terms of his ultimate ideals, he can take a stand.[13]

Weber continues:

> Now one cannot demonstrate scientifically what the duty of an academic teacher is. One can only demand of the teacher that he have the intellectual integrity to see that it is one thing to state facts, to determine mathematical or logical relations or the internal structure of cultural values, while it is another thing to answer questions of the *value* of culture and its individual contents and the question of how one should act in the cultural community and in political associations. These are quite heterogeneous problems. If he asks further why he should not deal with both types of problems in the lecture room, the answer is: because the prophet and the demagogue do not belong on the academic platform.[14]

As these passages show, Weber provides no set of concepts in the practical sciences analogous to the abstract ones in the theoretical sciences. He affirms the interaction of alternative perspectives based upon the ultimate value commitments of the protagonists, but he does not suggest any objective grounds upon which one may base a decision about competing values. As Weber puts it:

> . . . so long as life remains immanent and is interpreted in its own terms, it knows only of an increasing struggle of these gods with one another. . . . the ultimately possible attitudes toward life are irreconcilable, and hence their struggle can never be brought to a final conclusion. Thus it is necessary to make a decisive choice. . . .
>
> Science today is a 'vocation' organized in special disciplines in the service of self-clarification and knowledge of interrelated facts. It is not the gift of grace of seers and prophets dispensing sacred values and revelations, nor does it partake of the contemplation of sages and philosophers about the meaning of the universe.[15]

Weber makes a clear separation between ethics and science, speculative philosophy and theology. Ethics has no necessary relation to science, philosophy or theology, for ethics is the science which studies the "decisions" by which man clarifies his ultimate stand. Weber makes the following observation, for example, about the intellectual sacrifice which religious virtuosos must make:

> . . . For such an intellectual sacrifice in favor of an unconditional religious devotion is ethically quite a different matter than the evasion of the plain duty of intellectual integrity, which sets in if one lacks the courage to clarify one's own ultimate standpoint and rather facilitates this duty by feeble relative judgments.[16]

Weber's own interpretation—entirely consistent with his own understanding—is reflected in the following quotation:

> It is, however, no humbug but rather something very sincere and genuine if some of the youth groups who during recent years have quietly grown together give their human community the interpretation of a religious, cosmic, or mystical relation, although occasionally perhaps such interpretation rests on misunderstanding of self. True as it is that every act of genuine brotherliness may be linked with the awareness that it contributes something imperishable to a super-personal realm, it seems to me dubious whether the dignity

of purely human and communal relations is enhanced by these religious interpretations.[17]

Weber formulates two types of ethical views. On the one hand, man may affirm an ethic of conscience and decide for one Godhead. He damns the consequences of his decision by ignoring the fact that others are serving competing Godheads which produce behavior patterns whose consequences may be anticipated. Or, man may affirm an ethic of responsibility and take into account the probable consequences of his action. The anticipatable consequences of the actions of others condition his own decisions.

These distinctions may be compared with Weber's irrational and rational types of social action, although in this context, "non-rational" or "trans-rational" would perhaps be better terms than "irrational." In "Politics as a Vocation," Weber observes:

> . . . it is immensely moving when a *mature* man . . . is aware of a responsibility for the consequences of his conduct and really feels such responsibility with heart and soul. He then acts by following an ethic of responsibility and somewhere he reaches the point where he says: 'Here I stand; I can do no other.' That is something genuinely human and moving. And every one of us who is not spiritually dead must realize the possibility of finding himself at some time in that position. In so far as this is true, an ethic of ultimate ends and an ethic of responsibility are not absolute contrasts but rather supplements, which only in union constitute a genuine man. . . . [18]

Weber argues dialectically in his consideration of types of ethics. In the paragraph immediately preceding the above passage, he posits opposite types of ethics and ascribes qualities to each. He then observes that man unifies them by a decisive act of will. Weber's view of philosophy and ethics shapes his interpretation of theology and religion, which is discussed in the following section.

Weber's Understanding of Theology and Religion

Weber regards sacred values as the subject matter of the science of theology. They are a non-rational possession, for Weber has on principle rejected knowledge of such values.

. . . All theology represents an intellectual *rationalization* of the possession of sacred values. No science is absolutely free from presuppositions, and no science can prove its fundamental value to the man who rejects these presuppositions. Every theology, however, adds a few specific presuppositions for its work and thus for the justification of its existence. Their meaning and scope vary. Every theology, including for instance Hinduist theology, presupposes that the world must have a *meaning,* and the question is how to interpret this meaning so that it is intellectually conceivable. . . .

As a rule, theologies, however, do not content themselves with this (essentially religious and philosophical) presupposition. They regularly proceed from the further presupposition that certain 'revelations' are facts relevant for salvation and as such make possible a meaningful conduct of life. Hence, these revelations must be believed in. Moreover, theologies presuppose that certain subjective states and acts possess the quality of holiness, that is, they constitute a way of life, or at least elements of one, that is religiously meaningful. Then the question of theology is: How can these presuppositions, which must simply be accepted be meaningfully interpreted in a view of the universe? For theology, these presuppositions as such lie beyond the limits of 'science.' They do not represent 'knowledge,' in the usual sense, but rather a 'possession.' Whoever does not 'possess' faith, or the other holy states, cannot have theology as a substitute for them, least of all any other science. On the contrary, in every 'positive' theology, the devout reaches the point where the Augustinian sentence holds: *credo non quod, sed quia absurdum est.*

The capacity for the accomplishment of religious virtuosos—the 'intellectual sacrifice'—is the decisive characteristic of the positively religious man. That this is so is shown by the fact that in spite (or rather in consequence) of theology (which unveils it) the tension between the value-spheres of 'science' and the sphere of 'the holy' is unbridgeable.[19]

The ultimate validity of religion is based upon a non-rational "possession." The science of theology is the intellectual rationalization of this possession.

In Weber's view, science free from presuppositions, in the sense of freedom from religious bonds, does not know of miracle and of revelation. If science did acknowledge miracles or revelations, it would be unfaithful to its own presuppositions. In contrast, the believer affirms both miracle and revelation. Weber indicates the demand which science makes on the believer in this passage:

And science, 'free from presuppositions' expects from him no less—and no more—than acknowledgment that *if* the process can be explained without those supernatural interventions, which an empirical explanation has to eliminate as causal factors, the process has to be explained the way science attempts to do.[20]

Weber asserts that the believer can undertake this explanation without being disloyal to his faith. This affirmation is based on the fact-value disjunction which Weber presupposes. If this fact-value disjunction does not conform to man's fundamental experience, Weber is wrong when he advances this proposition.

Weber's fact-value dichotomy is similar to the one developed by many neo-Kantian Protestant theologians who maintain that God is "wholly other." They insist that man's reason cannot lead him to an understanding, confrontation, or experience of God; therefore, God must take the initiative to reveal Himself to man.

Weber's empirical studies and theoretic views are useful for those informed by this theological perspective, even though they ultimately differ on the question of an ontic dimension in the nature of things. His epistemological understanding, his emphasis upon the importance of man's will, and his ordering of the sciences are tantalizingly close to the views of a number of Protestant theologians.[21]

Weber distinguishes between religious philosophy and theology. Religious philosophy presupposes merely that the world has meaning, but theology adds other presuppositions to this one. As the nature of these additional presuppositions cannot be discerned *a priori*, one must examine the theology to see what additional presuppositions are added.

There is a close relation between the values which men hold and the religion which they follow. Weber's great interest in the scientific study of religion (in terms of his understanding of "scientific") is partly a result of this relation. His empirical studies of religious phenomena trace the interplay between values, social structures, and the decisions of men. Weber's conception of sociology as *verstehende* sociology coheres with this approach.

The Fundamental Informing Notions in Weber

The fundamental notions guiding Weber's social theory which have been delineated in the preceding two sections are summarized here. First, Weber posits a multiplicity of the sciences which is based on the perspective of man. The ordering of the sciences is guided by a movement from those phenomena most remote from man's organizing center to those closest to man's organizing center. Man is differentiated from sub-human species because he is a meaning-seeking, meaning-positing animal. This distinction permits Weber to make a fundamental division between the natural sciences and the social sciences; both, however, are theoretic sciences.

The subject matters of the natural sciences are the inorganic world and the sub-human part of man. Psychology is included in the natural sciences because it focuses not upon subjective meanings but upon physiological factors. The subject matters of the social sciences are focused on those elements in the social world in which subjective meaning is significant. The social sciences are differentiated by subject matter, time sequences, and perspectives.

Because meanings are always involved in human actions, the social scientist must always consider the culture which reflects men's subjective meanings. The social scientist *qua* social scientist is concerned with ethics, religious philosophy and theology because of the implications of the meanings embodied in them for men's actions. Cultural objects may be related either to man's necessities, as in the case of social, economic or political constructions, or to man's aesthetic or intellectual life.

Sociology is the most general social science; economics and political science deal with the economic and political orders. All are concerned with uniformities in empirical processes and are thereby differentiated from history which is concerned with individual and distinctive events. As it has been noted, psychology is a sub-human discipline. If psychologists explore questions of meaning, however, they are in the sphere of sociology according to Weber's ordering of the sciences.

Because of his rigorously phenomenological stance, Weber, unlike Kant and some of his successors, does not introduce an ontic notion of the Good into the practical sciences such as ethics and theology. Though Weber did not explicitly put the matter this way, a parallel to the practical sciences may be discerned in Weber's insistence that man must make a decisive choice to resolve questions of meaning. As there is no "oughtness" dimension necessarily present in his discussion of decisive choice, Weber cannot develop the extended exposition of the practical sciences which persons who add ontic or religious presuppositions undertake. Weber does locate theology among the sciences. It is the discipline which rationalizes the non-rational "possession" upon which religion is based.

Second, Weber makes the individual the ultimate locus of social action. Weber, unlike Durkheim, does not hypostatize society. It is actual human beings who are bearers of meaning and who act and respond to one another.

Weber distinguishes three types of social action, related to the degree of self-centeredness and self-consciousness involved in the action. Human actions may be mass, communal, or societal. Mass action, such as the mummering of workers in ancient China, is action in which the individuals have only a vague sense of common involvement. Communal action, such as the development of an initiation ritual for entry into a guild, is action in which the participants share common bonds which enable them to identify themselves as members of a common group. Societal action, such as the actions of a labor union to obtain economic benefits for its members, is action which is rationally directed toward the attainment of specified goals.

Reason (lacking ontological status), emotion and habit guide human action, which is rooted in acts of the will. Because man is a meaning-seeking, meaning-positing animal, sociology must be *verstehende* sociology and attempt to understand the meanings men ascribe to social action. Even if action is communal or mass, the social scientist must understand the values on which such action is based in order to interpret it.

Third, the fact-value cleavage and the related limitation of reason to technical and "logical" reason are fundamental in Weber's perspective. These distinctions and limitations permit Weber to argue for a "value-free" study of social phenomena. In a very real sense, the entire schema stands or falls on the adequacy of this understanding because it is this understanding which allows Weber to distinguish between the theoretical and the practical sciences and to minimize his own elaboration of the practical sciences. Weber overcomes the fact-value bifurcation by appealing to a decisive act of man's will, an act which establishes man's values.

Fourth, Weber traces the interplay between conflicting wills in the context of social-institutional configurations and value orientations. Weber orders this interplay by typological devices which he relates to historical data. He is especially interested in charismatic leaders because they are innovators and bearers of cultural traditions. This interplay between acts of men set in relation to social structures and values means the social scientist may expect to discern tendencies and configurations, but he should not expect to develop precise laws of human behavior.

In "Politics as a Vocation," for example, Weber traces the conflict of competing wills as he examines the processes by which modern states were unified. He sets this analysis in the context of different social-institutional configurations and value orientations in various countries. The configurations and values are themselves related to past decisions. Alliances between leaders in executive, military, legislative and judicial-bureaucratic structures are considered as Weber traces the way in which various states were unified.

A Critique

It is maintained here that the same fundamental categories are manifest in all creatures, so Weber's sharp distinction between the natural and the social sciences is rejected. Weber's distinctions are, nevertheless, based upon a proper contrast between the degree of feeling, meaning, and novelty of response displayed by men and other creatures of which we have some direct knowledge on this planet. Although the distinction between the natural and the social sciences is a matter of degree, the degree makes a great difference. All creatures in this cosmic epoch participate in the mathematical forms which make measurement possible, permit creatures to be located relative to other creatures, and contribute to their definiteness. Nevertheless, these mathematical relations, which are central in many of the natural sciences, are less important for the work of the social scientist who is primarily interested in the feeling tones, beliefs and actions of men which he relates to social structures. ("Feeling tone" is used to convey the notion that emotions involve valuation, purposiveness, and direction. Feeling tones, beliefs and actions are interrelated and mutually involve each other.)

Every creature is dipolar with both a physical pole, by which he appropriates forms of definiteness embodied in other creatures in the world, and a mental pole, by which he appropriates forms of definiteness embodied in the Divine. Each creature possesses a subjective aim, by which he decides what he is to be as he becomes. These common characteristics are contrasted with the degree of complexity of creatures and their capacity for novelty. Simple creatures, such as electrons, reproduce their past in the present with a modicum of change. Complex creatures, such as men, have complex feelings, a rich mental pole, and capacities for considerable novelty of response to their past as they become what they decide to be. These differences of degree mean that the proper methods for studying human beings are different than the proper methods for studying non-human subjects.

Vagueness is inherent in the study of the human being, because the intrinsic interrelatedness of the parts of a whole blurs the analysis. Man's capacity for novelty of response further limits the precision of social scientific "laws." The social scientist may expect to discern tendencies and configurations in his empirical investigations, but he should not seek highly precise laws of human behavior. That psychology which explores the feeling tones and meanings embedded in human beings should be given priority. The other social sciences are abstract sciences focused on part of the phenomena embedded in the feeling tones and structural relations of individuals.

The dipolar character of all creatures means that fact and value are inextricably interrelated. The forms of definiteness which the mental pole appropriates are embodied in the Divine Who urges creatures to become. Value is also embodied in other creatures in the world in whom an emerging creature participates as it begins to become. The Divine mediates aspects of other creatures to an emerging subject and supplements this physical objectification of one creature in another with alternative forms of definiteness as He lures the emerging subject-object into being. Every creature is both a subject and an object. It is a feeling subject as it becomes what it is to be; this decision to be involves some stamp of individuality, though in some cases it is very feeble. It is an object which is felt by other emergent subjects after it has become. Thus other creatures, God, and a decision by the emerging creature are involved in the becoming of every new creature.

This understanding, a return to pre-Kantian modes of thought, contrasts multiplicity or diversity with unity. Although there are multiple Godheads, there is also a universal lure toward harmony and intensification of feeling in which every entity participates. Therefore, the decision to become what one is—in Weber's terms, "to take a stand"—is more than simply an act of the will. The data involved in the decision do relate one to the universe; science may indeed be a way to true being, true art, true nature, true God or true happiness.

Weber rejects ontic reason, which has been understood classically as reason which participates in Being. Weber uses theoretic reason, which does not have ontic status for him, in sociological analyses. It is suggested here that reason is embodied in the primordial nature of God. Weber's explanation is incomplete, for an adequate understanding or explanation of experience involves an examination of the functioning of the Divine in the cosmos and of the participation of all creatures in ontic reason.

Although a theory of sense-perception is implicit in his fact-value dichotomy, Weber's treatment of the problem of perception is inadequate. Man cannot merely impose values upon objects because value is transmitted from objects to subjects. The theory of sense-perception which Weber implicitly presupposes ignores the massive earlier portion of sense data which is overwhelmingly emotive. It is true that a human being is prevented by finitude and ignorance from ever knowing a "thing in itself." It does not follow, however, that man knows nothing of a "thing in itself." Symbolic reference involves the interplay between man's experience and subject-objects. This complex interaction between symbols and events contributes to the great difficulty of assessing cause and effect relations in the social sciences.

Weber's emphasis upon man's will is distorted by his truncated understanding of power. Power understood as the ability to attain one's will in conflict with other wills emphasizes the importance of the disharmonious or competing dimensions of life. Weber ignores the over-arching lure for harmony also discernible in human experience. Although power includes compulsion, it also includes persuasion.

For example, in "Politics as a Vocation" Weber interprets the emergence of several modern states. He examines efforts of various political leaders to usurp power and considers the conditioning effects of different cultural conditions and social institutions configurations in the several countries. Although the importance and astuteness of Weber's analysis is great, a more extended consideration of the state's harmonizing and coordinating functions needs to be undertaken. Because of Weber's understanding of the nature of reality, this dimension, which is necessary for an adequate treatment of the state, is systematically excluded.

Weber refuses to define a state in terms of ends and defines it exclusively in terms of means. It is an entity having territory and a monopoly upon the use of power in that territory.

Weber properly notes that political actions are made by leaders who are ultimately responsible for them and that the leaders are frequently motivated by inordinate self-interest. Weber, however, does not adequately consider either the positive contributions which the state makes to the well-being of mankind or the differentials in excellence which the hierarchical ordering of people partially reflects. All power is not based merely on usurpation, as Weber suggests, even though part of it is.

The only judgment Weber can draw from his analysis of competing Godheads is that man must resolve the conflict by making a decisive choice. Weber cannot suggest ideal forms of social, economic, cultural, political or ecclesiastical organization to guide mankind in his quest for humanness. However, a consideration of the nature of man and experience can lead to some normative judgments.[22] Monogamy is the most desirable form of family organization; representative democracy, the most desirable form of political organization. Cultural and ecclesiastical pluralism and a "mixed" economic system are also normative. These affirmations permit an "isness-oughtness" contrast in sociological analysis, even though these ideal forms are not relevant in all contexts and can never be perfectly institutionalized in any context.

Weber displays a remarkable balance in relating universal factors to idiosyncratic factors in human affairs. The issue is cited to highlight the great difficulties encountered in assessing the relative importance of social structures, values, and wills in human life. The relation of universal factors to idiosyncratic ones is a perennial problem in the study of human beings. A whole is more than the sum of its parts because it is a new emergent; therefore, comparisons of different historical epochs and different cultures are only partially satisfactory. This problem is reflected in Weber's varied emphases upon man's will, upon ideal types, and upon his distinction between repeatable and non-repeatable ideal types.

Weber maintains a certain openness about religious experience and the expression of religious concern because of the limitations which he places upon reason. This openness and the phenomenological basis upon which he orders the sciences make him more congenial to certain theologians than either Durkheim or Parsons, but Weber's views make it extremely difficult to interpret religious experience on its own grounds. Those who affirm an interpenetration of fact and value must include such a subject-object in their analysis to develop an adequate interpretation of religious phenomena. A God Who is in some sense *sui generis* is needed.

The phrase "in some sense *sui generis*" is used to indicate that in some ways the Divine is independent of and unaffected by the world, but that in other ways God is dependent on and affected by the world. According to the interpretation of dipolar theism informing this discussion, God's primordial nature, His once-for-all envisagement of all potentiality, is unaffected by the world. In relation to His primordial nature, which is God's mental pole and is prior to His physical pole, God is *sui generis.* This side of the Divine nature is eternal and changeless. At the same time, His consequent nature, His everlasting objectification of the creatures of the world, is affected by the world. In relation to His consequent nature, which is God's physical pole and is subsequent to His mental pole, God is not *sui generis.* This side of the Divine nature is temporal and changing. Since God is a unity of the many creatures which constitute His consequent nature and of the forms of definiteness which constitute His primordial nature, He is "in some sense *sui generis.*" Alone by

Himself, deficient in actuality, He is *sui generis*, though this independence, conceivable by the exercise of negative judgment, is impossible in fact. Because of the universality of the principle of relativity, God is affected by the creatures of the world. In His actuality, God is partially dependent upon the world, so He is only qualifiedly *sui generis*.

Chapter VIII

Talcott Parsons' Ordering of the Sciences: A Resume and a Critique[1]

This chapter outlines the ordering of the sciences according to the analytical schema developed by Talcott Parsons in *The Social System*.[2] The bases of Parsons' classification of belief systems are examined. The fundamental notions undergirding the schema are suggested. Finally, these fundamental notions are criticized from an alternative perspective related to a different conception of the social studies.

Parsons' theoretical schema of the sciences of action is fundamentally inimical to the Christian tradition even if that tradition is interpreted broadly. It also contrasts sharply with a variety of alternative philosophical perspectives. These include neo-Kantian views, most adequately represented in sociology by Max Weber, and Platonic and Aristotelian approaches.

The importance of Parsons' theoretical schema of the sciences of action for social theorists informed by different understandings is twofold. First, it represents the most systematic formulation of social theory in contemporary American sociology. With great procedural clarity, Parsons presents a major way of viewing the world; by contrast, his schema also casts light on formulations more directly related to Christian perspectives and other philosophic viewpoints.

Second, the influence of this schema is so pervasive that an understanding of its fundamental assumptions is indispensable for anyone now working in the social studies. The widespread application of this schema to empirical investigations may produce difficulties for those who interpret the world from alternative perspectives, because investigators frequently permit the categories developed by Parsons and his colleagues to define inordinately the situation which they are examining. They often present their data at too high a level of abstraction, which precludes empathy with the feelings and cognitions of the people being studied.

In this chapter attention is confined primarily to parts of Parsons' major constructive work, *The Social System*, but some clarifying material drawn from *The Structure of Social Action* is also introduced.[3] The limitations involved in comparing passages from different works written in different periods and in different contexts should be borne in mind as the quotations from Parsons' earlier work are considered, for Parsons' systematic approach is not fully developed in *The Structure of Social Action*.

Although *The Social System* was published in 1951, neither Parsons' basic categories nor his analytical method have shifted significantly since that time. Although his later work offers some refinements and clarifications and further develops the implications of his schema, it does not suggest any fundamental changes in Parsons' approach and is therefore not explored here.

The descriptive portions of this chapter examine the ordering of the sciences and the types of belief systems which Parsons develops in *The Social System;* critical passages illustrating these notions are considered. Although a topical approach permits adequate treatment of the substance of Parsons' schema, it obscures facets of the structure of the argument. Proper treatment of the structural aspects of Parsons' work demands a far larger treatise. A structural examination would analyze Parsons' step-by-step process of construction as he combines fundamental elements with certain types of objects to produce new compounds which he then defines. The examination would show how he combines these new compounds with other elements or compounds to produce additional compounds, and so on, as he evolves a complex terminological and conceptual schema. The method of constructing a complex structure from simple parts can be traced to Democritus. Parsons' structural method accentuates the deterministic aspect of his work.

Parsons' Ordering of the Sciences

Parsons makes a fundamental division between "science" and "non-science." This latter area, including philosophy and theology, is "non-empirical" and is contrasted with "empirical science."

The methodological canons of science common to all "objects" of science permit a common scientific procedure. The varied "objects" of science—one might say a multiplicity of subject matters—produce a multiplicity of the sciences. However, as will be noted later, this multiplicity is ambiguous.

Parsons bases the fundamental division between "empirical" and "non-empirical" areas upon his understanding of "empirical" as that which involves "reality-testing" by cognitive or rational means. In this context, Parsons conceives reason as relatively limited "technical" reason. This meaning may be contrasted with the classic understanding of ontic reason which participates in being. Parsons' empirical ideas involve ". . . processes which are defined as subject to understanding and manipulation in a pattern of 'practical rationality,' that is, in terms of what we call empirical science and its functional equivalents in other cultures."[4]

Parsons interprets empirical science, in turn, as that corpus of knowledge which developed using four basic norms of scientific knowledge. They are:

(1) Empirical validity
(2) Logical clarity or precision of particular propositions
(3) Logical consistency of the mutual implications of propositions
(4) Generality of the "principles" involved, which may perhaps be interpreted to mean range of mutually verified implications.[5]

Two observations should be made about Parsons' enumeration of basic norms of scientific knowledge. First, he posits a common set of norms for the natural and the social sciences. This uniformity agrees with his earlier observation that common methodological canons apply to all the sciences. Second, the reader is left to puzzle about the meaning of "logical." The meaning may be inferred from the method of development which Parsons employs in *The Social System*, but he does not discuss it explicitly. Two passages from *The Structure of Social Action* may help to clarify the meaning of "logical."

In his critique of Max Weber's view of the methodological relations between the natural and the social sciences, Parsons argues that Weber should have affirmed that in a purely logical aspect there is no difference between them. Parsons says: "He [Weber] should have gone all the way to the view that in a purely *logical* aspect there is no difference whatever. The differences all lie on a substantive level."[6]

Because of this common logical aspect, Parsons considers analytic sciences in both the natural and the social sphere. Because of their relevance to the issue treated here and to the critique which will follow,

Parsons' observations in *The Structure of Social Action* are cited at some length. He writes:

> For the classification of the sciences the methodological arguments Weber has developed seem to indicate a basic division into two groups, substantially on the lines he has suggested, with a dominant direction of interest, on the one hand, toward the concrete individuality of one or a class of historical individuals and, on the other hand, toward a system of abstract general principles and laws. But this division does not coincide with that between the natural and the socio-cultural sciences. There are, rather, examples of both in each field. The first group may be called the historical sciences, which concentrate their attention on particular concrete phenomena, attempting as full an understanding of their causes and consequences as is possible. In doing this they seek conceptual aid wherever it may be found. Examples in the natural science field are geology and meteorology; in the social field, history, above all, but also anthropology as it has generally been conceived. [It will be noted that Parsons shifts his own characterization of anthropology between the time he wrote this passage and the time he wrote *The Social System.*] The other group, the "analytical," sciences, is concerned primarily with building up systems of general theory verifiable in terms of and applicable to a wide range of concrete phenomena. To them the individual phenomenon is a "case." In the natural science field theoretical physics is the leading example, but chemistry and general biology may also be included; in the social sciences theoretical economics is by far the most highly developed, but it is to be hoped that theoretical sociology and certain others will find a place by its side.

Parsons then adds the important clarifying footnote:

> Then for the historical sciences theoretical concepts are means to understanding the concrete historical individual. For the analytical sciences, on the other hand, the reverse is true; concrete historical individuals are means, "cases" in terms of which the validity of the theoretical system may be tested by "verification."
> From this is follows that there are two different possible meanings of the term "theory" which are often confused. On the one hand, we speak of the total explanation of a given concrete phenomenon, a historical individual or class of them, as a "theory," thus a "theory of eclipses" or Weber's own "theory of modern capitalism." On the other hand, we may apply the term to systems

of general concepts as such, thus the "Newtonian physics" or the "classical economics." Weber points out quite correctly that a theory in the second sense cannot *by itself* explain a *single* empirical fact. It requires *data* which are always empirically unique, are part of a concrete historical individual, for any concrete explanation or prediction.

Parsons continues in the text:

> These two types of sciences cut across each other in their application to fields of concrete phenomena. The same historical science will necessarily draw theoretical aid from a number of different analytical sciences, for example geology from physics, from chemistry and, in explaining the origin of organic deposits like coal, from biology. Similarly history should draw on biology, psychology, economics, sociology and other sciences. On the other hand, the theoretical system developed by an analytical science will normally be applicable to a number of different classes of concrete phenomena, for example physics to celestial bodies and the behavior of terrestial [*sic*] objects; economics to human actions in the market place and, in a less crucial role, to the church and the state. A distinction between the natural and the social sciences is possible on both levels. Historically considered the latter group is confined to the concrete phenomena of human life in social groups, analytically to those conceptual elements which are applicable only to this concrete subject matter.[7]

Parsons contrasts the methodological canons which apply to all of the sciences with the classes of objects of scientific investigation, for the differences between the several sciences emerge here. Parsons posits four classes of objects of scientific investigation:

(1) Physical objects, including organisms or "nature" (In some cases Parsons separates organisms from other physical objects.)
(2) Individual actors or personalities
(3) Collective actors or collectivities
(4) Cultural objects.

Thus Parsons develops a classification of the sciences based upon different objects of scientific investigation. This classification includes the natural sciences as a group, which Parsons would undoubtedly further differentiate if this area were his center of concern, and the sciences related to objects of interest to the theory of action. Parsons differentiates these sciences from the natural sciences because the objects of investigation entail a *re*action of alter. Parsons suggests that three sciences are comparatively independent because they are responsible for relatively distinctive conceptual schemata:

(1) The theory of personality systems
(2) The theory of social systems
(3) The theory of culture.

Parsons defines psychology as "... the science concerned with the elementary processes of action and their organization in personalities as systems."[8]

Sociology is the science concerned with institutions and institutionalization. In this context, Parsons raises the question of the status of economic and of political science. Because of its special focus upon what Parsons calls "instrumental evaluative action-orientation," which involves a decision by the actors in a given social system to select a rational or instrumental course of action, economic science has autonomous status as an analytical science in certain types of societies. As Parsons puts it:

> ... economics as a *social* science is concerned with the phenomena of rational decision-making and the consequences of these decisions within an institutionalized system of exchange relationships. This is, within the theory of action, such a highly distinctive complex that the claim of economic theory to autonomy with respect to it seems quite justified.[9]

Parsons rejects the notion that either political science or history possesses such autonomy; therefore, they are not analytical theoretical systems. Political science can make no such claim because power, its peculiar interest, is diffuse rather than specific. Parsons understands power as the ability to realize one's own values in conflict with others.

History is a synthetic discipline because it is not organized about a strictly limited set of variables. "It seems better," Parsons says, "to conceive history as a synthetic empirical science which is concerned with the mobilization of all the theoretical knowledge which is relevant in the explanation of processes in social systems and in cultural change in the past."[10] For the same reason, Parsons also categorizes population studies, "regional studies," and "international relations" as synthetic disciplines.

Distinctive sociological theory is "... *that aspect of the theory of social systems which is concerned with the phenomena of the institutionaliza- tion of patterns of value-orientation in the social system,* with the condi- tions of that institutionalization, and of changes in the patterns, with conditions of conformity with and deviance from a set of such patterns and with motivational processes in so far as they are involved in all of these."[11]

Parsons views social psychology as intermediate between sociology and psychology, for it does not have the same order of independent relations as psychology or sociology. It is not directly focused on the analysis of the structure of social systems, but is concerned with motiva- tions and personalities in their relation to and their interdependence with the structure of social systems.

Anthropology deals with the theory of culture which "... must be the theory concerned not only with the properties of culture as such but with the interdependence of patterns of culture with the other components of systems of action."[12] As noted earlier, this view clarifies the position which Parsons took in *The Structure of Social Action.* Parsons bases his delineation of anthropology on systematic considerations rather than on popular usage.

Parsons asserts that the disappearance of the major distinctions of his schema will mean that theory itself has evolved to a new level. This observation suggests that the multiplicity of the sciences which Parsons now envisions is due to a lack of scientific understanding. A unity of the sciences may develop with the growth of knowledge and theory.

Parsons maintains that the development of the social sciences involves the scientist's increasing capacity to predict and control human behavior in both the first and the last chapter of *The Social System.* In the first chapter, Parsons contrasts the unity of the underlying system of action with the diversity of the three types of objects. One may ask whether the diversity of objects would disappear with fully adequate scientific under- standing. As observed in Chapter VI, this issue dogged Emile Durkheim, one of the earlier theorists with whom Parsons has dealt so extensively.

Parsons argues that all scientific theory is concerned with the analysis of elements of uniformity in empirical processes. He states with approba- tion that "The essential question is how far the state of theory is devel- oped to the point of permitting deductive transitions from one aspect or state of a system to another, so that it is possible to say that if the facts in A sector are W and X, those in B sector must be Y and Z. In some parts of physics and chemistry it is possible to extend the empirical coverage of such a deductive system quite widely. But in the sciences of action dynamic knowledge of this character is highly fragmentary, though by no means absent."[13] This formulation is strongly reminiscent of the understanding of theory in classical mechanics, but it does not relate so adequately to field theory.

Types of Belief Systems for Parsons

The schema just reviewed is inextricably related to Parsons' classification of belief systems. He develops a fourfold typology of belief systems and contrasts non-scientific belief systems with scientific ones.

Belief systems are cultural objects. They constitute part of the subject matter of anthropology, one of the analytical sciences of action. According to Parsons, belief systems are one of three cultural pattern types. The other two cultural pattern types are systems of expressive symbols and systems of value-orientation.

Parsons bases this threefold classification on the three functional problem-contexts of action-orientation in general, which he argues are discerned in experience. They reflect themselves on the cultural level in three different cultural pattern types.

The first basic functional problem-context of action-orientation is cognitive. "Practical rationality," which Parsons refers to as "reality-testing," is dominant. That these notions are placed in quotations and are never defined in terms of anything else suggests that they are fundamental notions for Parsons. He appeals to concrete experience, but at this level the shape of his entire schema determines his conception of empirical experience. Parsons is referring to technical reason which is used to discern the most efficient means to a specified end. The cognitive problem-context expresses itself on the cultural level in belief systems.

As noted earlier, Parsons' understanding of reason may be contrasted with ontic reason, reason which participates in being. This ontological understanding is most frequently seen in the *logos* facet of the Christian Trinity and in the Platonic forms or eternal objects.

The second basic functional problem-context of action-orientation is emotional. Parsons refers to this context as the cathectic problem-context. It relates to the actor's emotive equilibrium which Parsons interprets by a gratification-deprivation balance. The cathectic problem-context expresses itself on the cultural level in systems of expressive symbols.

Parsons' understanding of the human psyche contrasts sharply with the understanding of most Christian social theorists, who interpret human emotion with the language of harmony and disharmony. This language, they think, is more able to describe fundamental human experience and its relation to the ultimate harmonizer of all diversity.

The last basic functional problem-context of action-orientation is evaluative. It arises because the actor must choose between alternative cognitive and cathectic components and between the dominance of cognitive and cathectic components. The evaluative problem-context expresses itself on the cultural level in systems of value-orientations.

Parsons identifies belief systems by the primacy of the cognitive functional problem-context of action-orientation. Granted this cognitive primacy, he then uses two fundamental categories of two components each to differentiate types of belief systems. He combines these components exhaustively to get four types of belief systems.

The first couplet of fundamental categories centers on the primacy of the cognitive or the evaluative component of the problem-context of action-orientation. Because cathectic orientation focuses about personality systems, it is subsumed by evaluative primacy at the cultural system level. Hence, only two of the three fundamental components of the problem-context of action-orientation are relevant for the classification of types of belief systems.

Parsons terms beliefs in which the cognitive component is primary "existential beliefs." The problem of truth is dominant here. He terms beliefs in which the evaluative component is primary "evaluative beliefs." The problem of meaning for the actor is raised here. This existential-evaluative couplet presupposes the discreteness of parts and a limited understanding of reason.

The second couplet of fundamental categories focuses about empirical and non-empirical beliefs. As noted earlier, for Parsons empirical ideas or beliefs ". . . concern processes which are defined as subject to understanding and manipulation in a pattern of 'practical rationality,' that is, in terms of what we call empirical science and its functional equivalents in other cultures."[14] By contrast, non-empirical beliefs are residual. They concern ". . . subjects which are defined as beyond the reach of the methodology of empirical science or its equivalent in the culture in question."[15] This empirical-non-empirical couplet presupposes the validity of Parsons' phenomenological understanding of cognition and a limited view of empiricism as well as the discreteness of parts.

Parsons then combines the cognitive-evaluative couplet with the empirical-non-empirical couplet to produce four fundamental types of belief systems:

(1) Empirical and existential belief systems, a special type of which are termed scientific belief systems
(2) Non-empirical and existential belief systems, termed philosophic belief systems
(3) Empirical and evaluative belief systems, termed ideological belief systems
(4) Non-empirical and evaluative belief systems, termed religious belief systems.

Two observations about this classification should be made. First, the residual and non-empirical status which Parsons ascribes to philosophic and religious belief systems effectively undercuts their capacity for formulating interpretive schemata or directing research in the social studies. This categorization bears a striking resemblance to the formulations of Democritus, Lucretius and some contemporary linguistic analysts. A. J. Ayer, a representative contemporary linguistic analyst, employs an analytical method directly comparable to Parsons' method: Ayer focuses upon words and their meanings; Parsons, upon objects allegedly discerned in "empirical reality."

Second, Parsons' distinction between evaluative and existential beliefs presupposes a fact-value disjunction which some traditions deny. To maintain this distinction, a theorist must establish the discreteness or the autonomy of parts. Parsons does this by isolating fundamental elemental components and objects. He then constructs the schema by combining them.

The reader may get some sense of the method Parsons uses to develop his schema from the discussion in this section. Note the types of definitions Parsons employs and the combination of the components Parsons makes to develop the typology of belief systems. Unfortunately, a full exposition of his method of construction can be adequately illustrated only by a sentence-by-sentence analysis of the text. As observed earlier, the topical treatment employed here does not permit a complete description of this aspect of Parsons' work.

The Fundamental Informing Notions in Parsons

The following informing notions are fundamental to the Parsonsian schema, which stands or falls on the adequacy and applicability of these notions.

First, the paradigm of interaction permits Parsons to make at least a provisional distinction between the natural and the social sciences. Out of this relational interactive system, Parsons delineates the three sciences of action—psychology, sociology and anthropology—centered upon psychological, social and cultural systems, respectively. Parsons defies a social system as "... a plurality of individual actors interacting with each other in a situation which has at least a physical or environmental aspect, actors who are motivated in terms of a tendency to the 'optimization of gratification' and whose relation to their situations, including each other, is defined and mediated in terms of a system of culturally structured and shared symbols."[16] As this definition indicates, Parsons discerns physical, social, cultural and psychical objects of the object world of the actor.

Second, the gratification-deprivation balance is fundamental to Parsons' interpretation of human motivation. Parsons' indebtedness to Freud is very great at this point.

Third, cognitive, cathectic, and evaluative modes of motivational orientation of action are posited. Parsons constructs his entire schema around these three fundamental concepts. As noted earlier, these concepts emerge out of the fundamental problem-context of action-orientation. Parsons relates cognitive orientation to technical reason which, guided by some type of means-ends schema, tests "reality." He interprets cathectic orientation through the use of the gratification-deprivation balance by which he understands human motivation. He characterizes evaluative orientation by the way in which an actor orders choices or selections between alternative cognitive and/or cathectic objects.

Fourth, Parsons' method of procedure is a method of construction. Parsons begins by isolating types of objects to help define fundamental concepts. He then builds the schema by combining and re-combining the fundamental concepts and objects. Often he defines the new compound resulting from the combinations. He then combines the new compound with other compounds or with other objects to produce another new compound, and so on. Parsons emphasizes precision of definition and clarity of procedure. He wants to get the scientist out of the picture and to attain "objectivity." The goal of all the sciences, including the sciences of action, is predicting the future state of the system and the components involved in it, given knowledge of the existing state of the system.

A Critique

Although the framework informing this critique contrasts sharply with Parsons', there are convergences at relatively low levels of abstraction. The convergences result from the universality of the cognitive, emotive and evaluative components which Parsons discerns in the fundamental problem-context of action-orientation.

Parsons' formulations are based upon a truncated triadic or Trinitarian understanding of the nature of reality. In classical Trinitarian terms, his cognitive, cathectic and evaluative components are analogous to the Son, the Father, and the Holy Spirit; in more general triadic formulations, to form, power and unification. Parsons' limited understanding of the nature of cognition and his judgment that these components are logically discrete accentuates the differences between Parsons and the view held here.

This critique focuses on four major issues. The inter-relatedness or the independence of the issues depends upon the analyst's understanding. It is maintained here that the issues are interrelated, so no priority is assigned to the sequence in which they are presented nor is any one issue more crucial than any other. The issues mutually support and imply one another.

First, the distinction between the several sciences is a matter of degree rather than a matter of kind as Parsons at least provisionally suggests, for the same fundamental categories are manifest in the realization of all entities. Parsons' distinction between physical, psychic, social and cultural objects cannot be sharply maintained because all entities involve a reaction with each other. At the same time, the degree of response varies markedly so a provisional distinction between the social studies and the natural sciences is legitimate.

From this point of view, the three analytical sciences of action which Parsons posits are abstractions from a concrete reality which is what it is. Structural components and articulated and formalized beliefs and values are fundamentally referable to the feeling tones of the individual persons who entertain them. Sociology, whose autonomy is provisional, focuses upon structural components. Anthropology, whose autonomy is also provisional, focuses upon articulated and formalized beliefs and values.

The unity of the sciences which Parsons seems to envision is one in which the knowledge of one state of the system and of its components would enable one to predict the future state of the system and of its components. As noted earlier, Parsons would view this emergent unity of the sciences as the evolution of theory to a new level. Such a unity might be attained in one of two ways. On the one hand, all knowledge might be reduced to a basic knowledge of bodies in motion or its equivalent. This development was anticipated by Democritus and finds contemporary expression in various forms of materialistic determinism. On the other hand, all knowledge might be raised to a basic knowledge of a sequence of ideas. This development was anticipated by Spinoza and finds contemporary expression in some Christian views of God's omni-science. On the basis of fully adequate knowledge either of things or of ideas, one could predict the future state of the entire system.

The unity envisioned here is a type which presupposes that the same fundamental categories are manifest in all entities. Knowledge of the present state of a system will not necessarily allow an analyst to predict future states of the system, for the past is not reproduced in the future without novelty. The uncertainty of such a prediction would be particu-larly apparent in the case of complex organisms such as human beings, but it would be true for all organisms in the long run. Plato reflects this perspective in the *Timaeus* when he observes that all nature can give is a likely tale. This unity may be contrasted with a diversity of the sciences due to the relative importance of the several categories and different forms of definiteness in various entities, but it is entirely appropriate to refer to the unity whenever useful in broader interpretive contexts.

Second, the gratification-deprivation balance by which Parsons inter-prets human motivation is rejected. Human motivation should be inter-preted in relation to a desire for aesthetic satisfaction and intensity of feeling. There are both internal and external sources of harmony and disharmony. The desire for aesthetic satisfaction is rooted in God's na-ture. Disharmony is caused by finitude, ignorance, and/or maliciousness.

This view of both internal and external sources of disharmony implies a denial of the Augustinian doctrine of original sin and a return to Pelagian alternatives. Substituting a harmony-disharmony balance for a gratification-deprivation balance represents a turn from a Freudian to a Platonic perspective. However, man's casual past clearly does condition his present, so, although it is recast, one of Freud's basic insights is affirmed.

Third, although the triadic view implied in Parsons' cognitive, cathec-tic, and evaluative components of action-orientation must be considered in any comprehensive schema, they need to be reformulated. Further-more, these components are intrinsically interrelated. The ultimate ap-peal here is to intuitive experience, for one cannot appeal to any notions more fundamental than these. This reformulation of cognitive, emotive and unifying components of experience and the affirmation that they are intrinsically interrelated imply a rejection of the fact-value distinction fashionable in contemporary social science and the logical-substantive distinction which Parsons posits.

Parsons' cognitive component should be extended to include ontologi-cal reason, for man's reason participates in the forms of definiteness which are encompassed in the primordial nature of God. Although emotion, or feeling tone, is elemental in experience, Parsons' cathectic component should be defined in terms of a harmony-disharmony balance rather than in terms of a gratification-deprivation balance, for this language more adequately points toward the experience of the lure for harmony and intensity of experience. Man does unify the emotional and conceptual aspects of experience as he decides to become. The decision to become is *sui generis*, but it arises out of a desire for aesthetic satisfaction which is grounded in the Divine.

The capacity for human novelty of response to the data man appropriates suggests a different goal for the social studies than the one which Parsons posits. As suggested earlier, Parsons' criterion for the validity of an analytic scientific theory is the extent to which the future state of the system may be predicted, given knowledge of the present state of the system. Man's increased understanding of the external factors contributing to human disharmony—psychic, social and cultural—should be used to reduce the disharmony; therefore, the goal of knowledge in the social studies should be to understand those factors limiting man's potential. Man should use such knowledge to assist him in appropriating more creatively that which he inherits. Man's novelty of response is such that configurations, patterns and tendencies are all that one can or should expect in the social studies.

Fourth, Parsons' degree of exactitude is fake. This judgment necessarily follows from two related ideas. First, since there is no categorical disjunction between physical, psychical, social and cultural objects, the distinctions between them are provisional. Second, cognitive, emotive and unifying components are intrinsically interrelated; a whole is more than the sum of its parts.

The inherent lack of exactitude and the importance of the idiosyncratic dimensions in human experience suggest that a social scientist should present research findings at relatively low levels of abstraction. This approach makes the findings more useful to those informed by alternative perspectives who may readily re-interpret the findings if they want.

Parsons' distinctions between various types of belief systems are suspect because fact and value are intertwined. The social scientist who ignores or dismisses fundamental ontological issues is doing so on arbitrary grounds.

When an investigator presents his data at higher levels at abstraction, he cannot ignore the truth of his interpretive schema. At these levels proponents of alternative perspectives encounter major disagreements. Some of the implications of one alternative perspective have been explored here and contrasted with the Parsonsian schema.

Chapter IX

Durkheim, Weber and Parsons:
Some Comparative Considerations

This chapter compares and contrasts the theoretical structures of Durkheim, Weber and Parsons.[1] All the schemata are important, since most contemporary sociologists who study religious phenomena have been influenced by one or another of these theoretical formulations. Although proponents of various theological viewpoints may find some dimensions of the work of all three theorists suggestive, most of them will not be satisfied with any of these theoretical schemata because none of them interprets religion as a *sui generis* phenomenon.

Parsons is farthest removed from the theological tradition of the West, for he emphasizes elements or components most antithetical to Christian perspectives. Although he does not espouse a confessional theology, Weber is useful to many confessional theologians for he is relatively open to a *sui generis* interpretation of man's inner history.

Durkheim, Weber and Parsons all envision a multiplicity of the sciences. Weber is unqualifiedly clear on this matter; Durkheim and Parsons are more ambiguous. Weber's multiplicity arises because man is related to and separated from the subject matter he is considering by his own perspectives. Durkheim's and Parsons' multiplicities arise because the several sciences study different objects. For these two theorists, the multiplicity of subject matters may be due either to different natures or to a lack of theoretical understanding.

Weber emphasizes the decisiveness of man's will in human action and consequently envisions a different relation between the individual and the community than either Durkheim or Parsons. He always analyzes the interplay between men's actions and the social structures created by limitations of nature, the past actions of men, and the meanings which men associate with their actions. The decisions of men are genuine factors in social life for Weber, who does not hypostatize society.

Durkheim encounters great difficulty with individuality, for he hypostatizes society and locates values there. He ascribes such great plasticity to the human being that it is difficult for him to establish any type of general norms or to hole up any form of social organization as an ideal for civilized mankind. Durkheim tries to resolve this dilemma by appealing to the scientist to discern whether shifts in norms are aberrations or appropriate responses to changing circumstances, but his efforts are not conclusive.

Parsons is closer to Durkheim than to Weber, for his criterion of predictive capacity to assess the adequacy of sociological theory implies a deterministic perspective. This perspective is incompatible with an understanding of human decision that includes novelty and genuine freedom as man responds to his world.

For Weber the elite group in a society is a power elite which can exercise its will or wills to attain its desired ends. This view guided his own interest in practical politics.[2] Durkheim and Parsons consider the social scientists as the elite group in a society, for scientists are most likely to understand and most able to explain the factors which have made things what they are.

None of these philosophical sociologists adequately explores the complex problems of human perception, but Durkheim probes this problem more intensively than Weber or Parsons. Weber interprets perception in neo-Kantian terms. He contrasts pure reason, through which man's categories of understanding are imposed upon data, with practical reason, through which man's ethical decisions are given form. Weber bases his fact-value dichotomy and his interpretation of theology on this dichotomy. Although he holds that man's decision is only partially conscious in many cases, Weber maintains a radical fact-value disjunction and suggests that man makes and affirms values only by acts of his will.

Both Durkheim and Parsons indicate that man discerns the objects in the world because of the force and constraint which they exercise upon him, so they appeal ultimately to the influence which the objects manifest. They are rigorously phenomenological on this issue; neither of them explores in detail any ultimate grounds for this influence. Durkheim does press the problem of perception more rigorously than Parsons, since he tries to show that society is the locus of concepts and the categories.

Durkheim and Parsons both attempt to "explain" values. Durkheim locates value in society; Parsons places it in the fundamental problem-context of action-orientation. Parsons interprets the emergence of values on the basis of the actor's selection between an array of alternative instrumental and cathectic components. Since Parsons uses a gratification-deprivation model to explain human motivation, he thinks that the actor's selection is guided by his efforts to maximize gratification.

Although Durkheim is more concerned with resolving coherently the question of the grounds for religious experience than Weber or Parsons, none of the three philosophical sociologists gives religious experience a *sui generis* character. Durkheim roots religious experiences in society; Parsons and Weber explain it by finitude and ignorance, the limitations of existence. Weber refuses to go beyond this characterization, for he bases religious affirmations upon man's decision to take a stand in favor of a religious point of view. Parsons undercuts the *sui generis* character of religious experience and attempts to explain religious phenomena on other grounds. His understanding of religious belief systems undermines the cognitive dimension of religious experience. Parsons explains the lure for religious experience by the gratification-deprivation balance in conjunction with the limitations of existence.

The methods which the three analysts employ differ markedly. In his empirical analyses Weber examines the interplay between competing wills. This examination is guided by typological formulations focused on structures and meanings. Although the formal side is important, Weber's emphasis on the interaction of human agents gives his analyses a dynamic character. Relatively open about the shape of emerging phenomena, Weber argues that tendencies and configurations are the most which one may seek in the social sciences. Because of his emphasis on meaning and human actions, he is sensitive to the distortions which typological analyses can impose upon historical data.

Durkheim's treatment of origins is more analytical and deterministic than Weber's. When Durkheim wants to understand the origins of a phenomenon, he breaks down the emergent compound into the elements or simpler compounds which compose it. This approach permits Durkheim to make refined statistical comparisons between various components.

However, Durkheim also allows for the relative autonomy of emergent phenomena, so he uses two approaches. The first approach reduces a whole to the parts comprising it; the second approach traces the interplay of parts in a given sphere. He uses the former method in his elaborate morphological analyses and in his studies of origins. He uses the latter method in his treatment of the structural relations between the sciences and between individual and collective representations and in his discussion of the spontaneity of collective representations.

Parsons uses a rigorous method of construction, as the careful and systematic development of a whole out of simpler parts has been termed here. This method permits Parsons and persons using his schema to make elaborate cross-cultural and intergroup comparisons.

This chapter concludes the examination of these seminal philosophical sociologists. Part Four explores alternative theological perspectives on the nature of reality. Readers whose constructive views are guided by any of the sociologists considered here will inevitably raise critical questions about the shape of the analyses and the typological devices employed in Part Four, for the analyses are focused upon views which presuppose a God Who is at least partially *sui generis* and transcendent.

The analyses in Part Three have explored alternative phenomenological or reductionist interpretations of religious phenomena; the analyses in Part Four consider alternative ontic or *sui generis* interpretations. These contrasting analyses are designed to demonstrate the internal power of alternative interpretations of religious phenomena. If an investigator presents his research findings at relatively low levels of abstraction, translating the data from one interpretive framework to another may be easy; but if he has permitted his conceptual framework to shape his data inordinately, the translation may be difficult or impossible.

Because a research worker's interpretive framework inevitably affects the tone of his presentation, no translation from one framework to another is completely satisfactory. However, a research worker may deal more empathically with the inner meaning of religious experience if his theoretical views permit him to interpret the phenomenon in a *sui generis* manner. Although the social scientist may minimize these difficulties provisionally by presenting his data at a low level of abstraction, he must ultimately appeal to a more general schema as he identifies, studies and interprets phenomena which he alleges are religious. At this level some disagreements between social scientists who entertain phenomenalistic or reductionist views and social scientists who espouse ontic views are inevitable.

PART FOUR

Theological Interpretations,
Typological and Constructive

Chapter X

Some Methodological Reflections on the Social Scientific Investigation of Sermonic Discourse and Religious Experience

Part Four is focused more directly upon theological issues than the other parts of this book. This chapter reviews the salient dimensions which must be considered in the social scientific investigation of sermonic discourse and religious experience. Because the guiding principles are quite general, the methodological issues are relevant to other subject matters.

In spite of the emphasis upon preaching among many contemporary Protestant theologians and in spite of the importance of the sermon in Protestant public worship, social scientists have made few studies of sermonic discourse. Neither the types of sermons which religious professionals deliver nor the appropriations which laymen make of them have been studied intensively. Such studies would increase understanding of the communication of religious symbols and ideas and might contribute to the improvement of contemporary preaching.

This chapter explores three dimensions of the question. The first two sections examine alternative inner meanings of sermonic discourse and religious experience and delineate alternative approaches to the study of sermons. The first section considers the effects of alternative theoretical perspectives upon the shape of research efforts and the interpretation of sermonic discourse and develops a constructive view of the shape such research should take. The succeeding section considers the way in which alternative epistemological principles condition one's view of the nature of sermonic discourse and religious experience in order to illustrate alternative perspectives affirming a God Who possesses at least some transcendent and *sui generis* characteristics. The final section examines the relation between linguistic symbols and experience. Although the discussion is focused upon the implications of this relation for the interpretation of sermonic discourse, it is of general significance because so many social scientific studies are based upon linguistic data.

Perspectives on Sermonic Discourse: Analytic and Constructive

Those who assume a radically existential, phenomenological stance see no difference between sermonic discourse and any other mode of argumentation, for they assess the impact of any speech by its effects upon the hearers and base their evaluation of it upon the hearer's self-report and upon their observations of his actions or responses. Extreme protagonists of this perspective would not even explore conditioning factors which others might think significant; all proponents of this perspective would resist any efforts to relate the sermon to a transcendental referee and fundamental religious experience.

Since it is held here that social scientific findings should be presented at a low level of abstraction, any research effort which does not incorporate this existentialist perspective is inadequate. Although other dimensions must be included, this type of analysis is the first task. Many theological discussions of sermons obscure contingent and differentiable dimensions because they are developed at too high a level of abstraction.

Investigators who are persuaded that underlying factors determine human behavior will focus extensively upon these particular components as they explore the appropriation of sermonic discourse. They will rigorously examine an array of attitudinal factors and such structural components as age, sex, status, ethnic and family background, residence, religious affiliation, and level of education. A research worker's views of the autonomy of the parts of a whole and of the extent of man's capacity to respond novelly condition the intensity of his analysis and his treatment of a range of variables. Psychologists informed by Freudian perspectives and sociologists informed by Durkheimian and Paretoian perspectives would press this approach rigorously.[1]

Examination of these conditioning dimensions is important because emerging entities do appropriate elements from the past as they become. Those events which have become are in the past and are mediated to an emerging entity through the activity of God. Because of different perspectives, different events have different pasts so the past of one event may be the present of another. However, these subtleties may usually be ignored in the study of social phenomena.

Although they are "back" of experience and condition the present, these events do not determine the present. Social scientific analysis of the factors conditioning human behavior is useful, but the novelty inherent in man's decisions and the contextual character of experience limit the usefulness of casual analysis.

Man's ability to reflect upon social scientific studies highlights the importance of the "feed-back" process in social research. Although finitude, ignorance and inertia limit man's capacity to respond, he may use social scientific studies to assist him to respond more responsibly and creatively to existing conditioning dimensions of life and to transform some of those which cripple him.

Protagonists who see the sermon in the context of social institutional configurations are closely related to this casual perspective, but they would allow for a greater flexibility of human response. This approach is congenial to Roman Catholic views, for proponents may argue that some levels of experience may be examined independently of an explicit experience or understanding of the Divine. Proponents might hold that for certain carefully delineated purposes one should consider the social institutional configurations which condition both the form of sermonic discourse and the extent of lay appropriation. Proponents may relate this approach to a higher understanding in which they relate the sermon to true Being. They would reject any interpretation which suggested unqualifiedly that the effects of the sermon on the listener are a consequence of social institutional factors.

Protagonists of Roman Catholic perspectives would supplement this Aristotelian perspective by appealing to God's self-revelation which illuminates facets of the service of Divine worship and gives preeminent position to the Mass. The dominance of form and the specificity of God's revelation in Jesus Christ mediated by the Holy Catholic Church in some Roman Catholic views produce an interpretation which many find arbitrary and authoritarian.

Social institutional factors must be considered in the study of sermonic discourse, but they are abstractions and simplifications of the concrete network of relations between human beings. Persons who reify these abstractions develop analyses which are too formal and too static. Although sympathetic to Roman Catholic views which relate the worship service to a reality which is at least partially *sui generis* and transcendent, the viewpoint held here rejects the formalism and the specificity of the locus of revelation of most Catholic views.

Protagonists of the last perspective considered here affirm a Divine reality which is actually or potentially inextricably related to sermonic discourse.[2] Proponents of some variants of this view think that the analyst who interprets the sermon in the same way he interprets any other form of discourse commits a radical error. Others make a sharp distinction between the internal appropriation of sermonic discourse and the external study of it, but hold that both views are legitimate. Some maintain that sermonic discourse embodies some elements in common with other modes of experience, but that it also has special qualities. Still others see only a difference of degree between sermonic discourse and other modes of argument. All proponents of this broad view maintain that an analysis of sermonic discourse which ignores the Divine reality is inadequate.

An adequate study of sermons should consider both the factors which affect their shape and their appropriation and the Divine reality which is the ultimate lure and referee of sermonic discourse. The investigator's interests, resources, and audience may help him determine the dimensions he includes and the balance he maintains between them. Because a broader consensus can be attained about the study of the factors conditioning sermonic discourse than about the ultimate referee and lure of it, a sociologist may want to confine himself to these conditioning factors. His decision, however, is arbitrary as there is no clear dividing line between the areas.

This chapter is especially concerned with alternative Protestant views of the way in which man becomes aware of or experiences the Divine, for man's interpretation of sermonic discourse is guided by his understanding of this problem. One useful way of approaching this issue is to examine epistemological options reflecting different views of God-man relations.

Epistemological Options and Normative Interpretation of Sermonic Discourse

Three relations between reason and perspectives which affirm a Divine reality are possible. Protagonists' views of God-man relations, the nature of religious experience and sermonic discourse, and the nature of man are intimately related to these epistemological options.

Proponents of the first option affirm that reason may penetrate to the nature of things, but not all of them equate Being and reality. Protagonists of the second option see a relation but not a correspondence between man's reason and reality. Supporters of the third option see no relation between man's unredeemed reason and his capacity to understand the ultimate character of reality.

Those who maintain the first option usually have a Pelagian understanding of sin, so they appeal to finitude, ignorance and lethargy to interpret man's experiences of disharmony and his inability to apprehend and respond to the Divine lure. Although proponents frequently qualify their views, persons who hold the second option customarily entertain some doctrine of original sin. They hold that man's experience of disharmony and his inability to respond to God's will is due to a fault in man's internal disposition, for man lacks adequate trust in God. Proponents of the third option customarily affirm a radical doctrine of man's total depravity and see no point of contact between man and God prior to God's revelation of Himself to man, because man's willful self-centeredness has obscured his relation to the Divine.

In this discussion each option is illustrated by a passage from a contemporary philosopher or theologian. The three thinkers are engaged in a family quarrel, for they hold sufficient presuppositions in common to permit some interchange. Each acknowledges a Divine reality Who is, at least in part *sui generis* and transcendent, affirms man's internal freedom, and sets his analysis in the context of a harmony-disharmony contrast.

Those who hold that reason can penetrate to the Divine reality discern an intrinsic reasonableness in the nature of things. Contrary to the way in which some opponents have interpreted this view, proponents do not necessarily equate reason with being and being with reality. They may also hold that finitude and ignorance preclude the development of a fully adequate metaphysical system and that dynamics is more fundamental than form.

Protagonists of this view maintain that any experience has the potential of illumining the fundamental structure of all experience and that therefore revelation is universal. To develop a general interpretive framework, a theorist has to draw from his particular concrete, unique experience, for, although he may think about universal, abstract concepts, he does so through his own experience. Proponents of this option may hold that reflective persons nurtured in the complex of meaning and feeling of any major religious tradition may choose to remain in their tradition, but they would deny the unequivocal, unique character of the conceptual formulations informing any religious tradition. At an appropriate level of generality, the conceptual schema of a particular religious tradition should reflect similarities with conceptual schemata drawn originally from other concrete data. If the conceptual side of a tradition does not reflect these similarities, they believe it should be revised so that it does so.

Many rationalists desire and anticipate a convergence toward a common understanding of the nature of God from a variety of religious traditions and so-called secular disciplines. This common understanding of God and His character in the history of mankind should coordinate the views about His nature and character developed by Christianity and other religious traditions.

Alfred N. Whitehead, who exemplifies one version of this first option, expounds his faith in rationalism in this passage:

> That we fail to find in experience any elements intrinsically incapable of exhibition as examples of general theory, is the hope of rationalism. This hope is not a metaphysical premise. It is the faith which forms the motive for the pursuit of all sciences alike, including metaphysics.
>
> In so far as metaphysics enables us to apprehend the rationality of things, the claim is justified. It is always open to us, having regard to the imperfections of all metaphysical systems, to lose hope at the exact point where we find ourselves. The preservation of such faith must depend on an ultimate moral intuition into the nature of intellectual action—that it should embody the adventure of hope. Such an intuition marks the point where metaphysics—and indeed every science—gains assurance from religion and passes over into religion. But in itself the faith does not embody a premise from which the theory starts; it is an ideal which is seeking satisfaction. In so far as we believe that doctrine, we are rationalists.[3]

Whitehead's view of the relation between reason and a transrational moral intuition permits him to interpret the lure of reason and to discern the limitation of reason in illuminating the nature of things. One must always remember the relation of reason to experience in this kind of rationalism; for this relation, coupled with the inadequacy of words to penetrate the nature of experience and with human finitude and ignorance, limits the adequacy of any metaphysical formulation.[4]

Thinkers who employ the second epistemological option see a relation between reason and a transcendent reality: although some understanding of the ultimate nature of reality is revealed in the common experience of mankind, God must initiate a unique revelation to man to reveal His ultimate character. Christian theologians who exercise this option frequently distinguish between general revelation, the aspect of revelation available to all men, and special revelation, the revelation of God in Jesus Christ.

Proponents of the distinction between general and special revelation may base it upon three factors which they may hold independently or in some combination. They may maintain that a blemish in man's nature obscures man's awareness of the Divine, that the dominance of dynamics over form focuses revelation upon a concrete encounter, or that a clear differentiation exists between understanding available to every rational creature and that available because of God's self-revelation to man. The first and third factors have been cited most frequently in Catholic theological formulations; the first and second factors have been employed most frequently in Protestant theological formulations.

The contemporary Protestant theologian, Reinhold Niebuhr, for example, holds that the understanding of God as Creator and as Judge may be discerned in the common experience of mankind but that His character as Redemptive Love is peculiarly revealed in Jesus Christ. He suggests the notion of the Hidden Christ who may be discerned by those who do not know Christ after the flesh in order to retain the character of special revelation but to generalize it beyond a particular historical tradition. Niebuhr advances one version of this second major epistemological option in this passage:

> . . . We thus have in the problem of human nature one of the many indications of the relation of general and special revelation, which concerns theology so perennially. The conviction that man stands too completely outside of both nature and reason to understand himself in terms of either without misunderstanding himself, belongs to general revelation in the sense that any astute analysis of the human situation must lead to it. But if man lacks a further revelation of the divine he will also misunderstand himself when he seeks to escape the conditions of nature and reason. He will end by seeking absorption in a divine reality which is at once all and nothing. To understand himself truly means to begin with a faith that he is understood from beyond himself, that he is known and loved of God and must find himself in terms of obedience to the divine will. This relation of the divine to the human will makes it possible for man to relate himself to God without pretending to be God; and to accept his distance from God as a created thing, without believing that the evil of his nature is caused by this finiteness.[5]

Theologians who entertain the third epistemological option deny any relation between man's unredeemed reason and ultimate reality; man's awareness of the nature of God is a result of His revelation to man. Initiated by the Divine, this encounter between man and God establishes a knower-known relation based upon what may be called a theo-volitional epistemological principle.

Christian theologians holding this alternative locate man's understanding of the character of God in the unique revelation in Jesus Christ, and in the Bible, the history of God's people, the Church, and the personal experience of the believer, who is differentiated from the non-believer by the presence or absence of this inner experience. They emphasize the particularity of the Christian faith and the radical discontinuity between this and any other experience.

Proponents who emphasize the dominance of form stress certain books, rites, or institutions which they think may lead mankind to the Divine, but proponents who emphasize the dominance of dynamics accentuate the concreteness of the encounter between man and God and contrast the external vehicles of the encounter with its internal meaning. Both so-called Biblical fundamentalists and neo-orthodox theologians such as Karl Barth and Richard Niebuhr, for example, emphasize the uniqueness of the Bible and the rites of the Christian Church; but fundamentalists maximize the significance of the written form through which the revelation is conveyed. In respect to the dominance of form, an intriguing relation exists between Biblical fundamentalists and Roman Catholicism.

Emil Brunner formulates his version of this third epistemological option in this passage:

> The task of ethics, like that of theology as a whole, is rather negative than positive: to clear away the difficulties raised by our own minds which prevent us from understanding the message.[6]

Protestants, who stress dynamics rather than form in man's relation to the Divine, are guided by one of these epistemological options when they define sermonic discourse. Protestants who affirm that reason can penetrate to the nature of reality hold that any discourse which explores the systematic interrelatedness of ideas or evokes intuitions of the Ultimate Unifier of ideas and Receptor of experience possesses sermonic dimensions. All is referred to Him and all is mediated by Him. Although in certain contexts a proponent may think a sermon should be more evocative than cognitive, he does not distinguish on principle between the sermon and any other mode of rational discourse. Therefore, preachers are teachers, but in worship contexts a religious professional should be sensitive to the evocative power of religious symbols and to the appropriateness of his observations for the context in which he finds himself. For Protestant proponents who think evocative and cognitive dimensions of experience are intertwined, all religious symbols, including the linguistic ones used in sermons, may evoke religious experience.

Protestants who distinguish between general and special revelation maintain that sermonic discourse is both expository and evocative. The expository dimension is rooted in the common religious experience of mankind; the evocative dimension, in God's revelation of Himself to the worshiper.

Protestants who affirm the radical disjunction between God and man argue that the sermon is unqualifiedly evocative. The religious professional confesses God's revelation and elicits the community's memory of its history. The worshiper's experience of the Divine is given shape by shared symbols, but it is a consequence of the Divine initiative. Persons who affirm this option are apt to be strongly Bible-centered. Since the Bible provides the forms through which witness is given, the sermon has a proclamatory and confessional character.

Linguistic symbols are inherently ambiguous. The final section of this chapter explores the reasons for this ambiguity and considers the implications of this ambiguity for the social scientific study of religious phenomena.

Linguistic Symbols, Religious Experience and Social Scientific Study: A Constructive View

The interpretation of the linguistic symbols which mediate, shape, and communicate experience between men is based upon an individual's conception to which the symbols relate. Some hold that all linguistic symbols only elicit emotions from the hearer. Others maintain that some linguistic symbols are purely emotive, some purely cognitive, and some both emotive and cognitive. Still others insist that all linguistic symbols are both cognitive and emotive.

Linguistic symbols are ambiguous because of the inferential relation between words and experience. Since a variety of linguistic symbols may refer to an experience, a particular symbol may be a more significant bearer of meaning for one individual than for another. Differences in men's understanding of the relations between symbols and the experiences to which they refer are a perennial source of misunderstanding and disharmony. However, this misunderstanding and disharmony may be reduced and more poignant symbols may be developed by a more adequate examination of the experiences to which the symbols refer.

If two or more people participate in much common experience, their shared linguistic symbols may evoke rich emotive experiences, so they may fruitfully use symbols laden with emotional overtones and highly specific references in their communication. However, if two or more people share little common experience, such symbols will not evoke emotive responses, so they will have to employ more general symbols related to broader backgrounds of experience in order to communicate effectively.

Linguistic symbols cannot communicate completely because no two men have exactly the same experience and because their experience begins with the selective appropriation of data drawn from their past. The first factor means that men's shared symbols never refer to precisely the same experience. The second factor suggests that a changing relation between linguistic symbols and the experience to which they refer is a perennial phenomenon and that linguistic symbols never exhaust the meaning which may be derived from an event. Men may add new meanings to old symbols because of changes in their own understanding.

This experience of men may be contrasted with the experience of God. Because His conceptual experience is both inexhaustible and prior to His physical experience, He is able to retain perfectly and everlastingly all that the world has to offer to Him. Although the symbols which other entities use affect the Divine Life, He Himself has no need for anything analogous to linguistic symbols; He retains the past perfectly and is able to contrast it supremely with the emergent present.

Every symbol conveys both emotive and cognitive meaning. The dual character of symbols is related to the nature of the experience to which all symbols refer, for all experiences embody both cognitive and emotive components. Because every emotion evokes conceptual feelings in its recipient and because every conceptual feeling elicits emotional feelings in its recipient, symbols which are dominantly emotional may evoke conceptual feelings. Conversely, symbols which are dominantly conceptual may arouse rich emotive feelings in the recipient. Anyone who has mastered an especially difficult intellectual problem may empathize with this observation.

Although all experience involves the integration of conceptual and physical feelings as an entity becomes what it is to be, religious experience is experience in which an individual harmonizes conceptual and physical feelings as he grasps and is grasped by a vision of the true, the good, and the beautiful inherent in the nature of things. Because these components are intertwined, any cognitive, moral, or aesthetic experience may elicit religious experience. Those who hold that any human experience has the potential to illumine the nature of things cannot distinguish sharply between sermonic discourse and other modes of human expression.

These considerations clarify the difficulties encountered in social scientific studies of the meanings embedded in religious symbols and sermonic discourse. Social scientists may examine the form and content of sermonic discourse in religious institutions to discern similarities and differences between the forms sustaining various religious traditions, to gain insight into the value orientation of religious elites, and to evaluate lay appropriation of sermonic discourse; but the degree of precision which can be attained is limited by the nature of the subject matter. One is not even certain *a priori* where to begin an investigation since genuine religious experience may occur anywhere.

Because of these intrinsic problems all social scientific efforts to probe religious experience are tentative: religious experience is more fundamental than any of the abstractions made from it in social scientific studies. The individual cannot articulate adequately the nature of his experience, and there are infinite shades of intensity of feeling and meaning in religious experience.

Research instruments are least adequate in investigations of the nature of religious experience itself. Religious sentiments and feelings are somewhat easier to explore, although the problems of symbolic reference and the locus of religious experience limit research efforts in this area. Since cognitive structures and explicit beliefs are more public, they are relatively easier to investigate. Interactive patterns and social-institutional configurations are most public, so they are studied most readily.

Although these difficulties are greatest in the study of religious experience, they extend to all social scientific investigations of attitudes, beliefs, and interactive patterns; vagueness characterizes much of the empirical data used in sociological and psychological research. A research worker who subjects interview or questionnaire data to rigorous and highly refined analysis is strongly tempted to think that he knows more than he does. This danger is increased if the data are subjected to numerous cross-analyses in which the language of "dependent" and "independent" variables is employed to suggest some kind of causal or quasi-causal relationships between the factors. In fact, the variables are inextricable intertwined and it is impossible to show conclusively which variables are dependent and which independent. This difficulty is compounded because important aspects of the sustaining environment are either completely presupposed or systematically excluded in some analyses and because novel and emergent factors constantly reshape the meanings and feelings which linguistic symbols elicit.

These problems are illustrated by Gerhard Lenski's *The Religious Factor* and Charles Y. Glock's and Rodney Stark's *Christian Beliefs and Anti-Semitism*, two of the most celebrated works in the sociology of religion to appear recently in the United States.[7] Both works qualifiedly affirm the dominance of form over dynamics in human affairs and religious experience. They attempt to construct indices of religious belief to which they relate other formal factors as they try to trace "causal" influences. They fail to consider the contributions of culture-bearing "creative minorities," who are so important in conditioning and shaping the emerging life of a society. Indeed, their narrow definitions of religious orthodoxy would exclude most Christians of this type.

Lenski is thus led to predictions about religious compartmentalization in the United States which are in marked contrast to the actual course of historical events; Glock and Stark convey a false precision in their discussion of the relation between Christian beliefs and anti-semitism and deal inadequately with Christianity's contribution to the quest for human brotherhood. Human life and religious experience cannot be embalmed in the manner which these methodologies encourage.

Chapter XI

The Nature of Religious Institutions and the Role of the Religious Professional: Analytic and Constructive Perspectives

Every social scientist who studies religious institutions and every religious professional who serves them confronts the question of the adequacy of his informing schema. Their identification and interpretation of the "religious" institution and their view of the relation of religious institutions to culture and to forms of social organization are shaped by their frameworks.

Although social scientists may minimize the consequences of differences between alternative perspectives by presenting research findings at low levels of abstraction and by seeking relatively neutral categories of analysis, they cannot eliminate the effects of such differences. Every author must make decisions about the inclusion or exclusion of normative materials, about the shape and tone of a research monograph, about individual and group whole-part relations, and about the relation of religious institutions to other forms of social organization. Social scientists who employ fashionable empirical-non-empirical and/or fact-value distinctions make many explicit or implicit judgments about the nature of perception and ignore complex fact-value problems related to the mediation of data embodied in one entity to another entity.

Because it is maintained here that fact and value are inextricably intertwined, both analytic and constructive material are incorporated. This chapter delineates alternative perspectives on the fundamental nature of religious phenomena, traces the implications of these perspectives for the understanding of the nature of the religious institution, considers the role of the religious professional in alternative *sui generis* perspectives on the fundamental nature of religious phenomena, and advances a constructive interpretation of God-world relations, the nature of the church, and the role of the religious professional in contemporary American society.

The delineation of the institution termed a religious institution, a religious collectivity, or a church commits a sociologist—at least implicitly —to one of the broad interpretative perspectives discussed here. Therefore, the exploration of alternative theological perspectives in this chapter is more than a rehearsal of obscure and irrelevant theological questions. Although they may not agree on the framework which they use to guide the gathering and ordering of data on religious phenomena, both social scientists and religious professionals are necessarily involved in seeking an adequate interpretation of religious phenomena.

As human beings are meaning-seeking, meaning-positing creatures, these issues are important for the life of both the religious institution and civilized mankind. Man may be effected directly by social scientific studies about him unlike the objects of natural scientific studies.

The typology used to order the discussion in the following two sections is based upon the notions of form and dynamics and upon their unification in one Supreme Entity and in many other entities. It reflects the shape which formal, efficient, final and material causes take in the perspective of process philosophy. Since the notions guiding the formulations developed here are general ones, their qualified emergence in a variety of alternative informing perspectives may be anticipated.

The distinctions between alternative God-world relations and between alternative theistic interpretations of the religious institution are guided by the geometric relations of identity, overlap, contiguity and independence. These relations are probably the most general relations possible between two entities.[1]

The following section considers alternative interpretations of the nature of religious phenomena. Because internal interpreters of religious institutions base their understanding of them on theological interpretations, these alternatives are explored in considerable detail.

Social scientists who maintain that understanding the belief systems of the members of religious institutions is a necessary part of their investigations will have to consider the views of the culture-bearing and culture-shaping elites within those institutions. Some of them may also be persuaded of the validity of one or another of the theological perspectives. Unless such social scientists can affirm the fact-value disjunction associated with the neo-Kantian tradition of men such as Ernst Troeltsch, Max Weber and H. Richard Niebuhr, they either must incorporate a theological viewpoint in their interpretive frameworks or must order their data by frameworks which interpret religious phenomena on other grounds.

Although many social scientists will agree that explanation rather than description is the aim of the social scientific study of religious institutions, they disagree sharply about the style and shape of an adequate explanation. Some will hold that an adequate explanation must include a consideration of the Divine subject-object which fosters the emergence of the religious institution. Others reject such interpretations as "prescientific" or as based on a fundamental misunderstanding of the scientific method. The second section explores the shape of alternative characterizations and explanations of religious institutions.

Some social scientists with strong empirical interests and some theologians who emphasize the dynamic side of experience may object to the formal analysis advanced in these sections, but the only genuine alternatives to at least limited formal analysis are impressionistic and undisciplined formalizations guided implicitly by one or more of the broad perspectives delineated here.

The structure of the following two sections is outlined in Figure 1. The diagram may help the reader to follow the discussion and to discern the basic assumptions shaping the ensuing presentation.

The third section considers the role of the religious professional from a point of view which enables protagonists to affirm the *sui generis* character of religious institutions.

The final section presents a constructive perspective on God-world relations, the nature of the Church, and the role of the religious professional in contemporary American society.

Alternative Perspectives on Religious Phenomena

As noted previously, there are four broad alternative perspectives from which one may interpret the character of religious phenomena.[2] One of these options affirms a transcendent or "depth" dimension of experience or some understanding of a "world behind the world" thereby maintaining the *sui generis* nature of religious experience. Proponents of the other three viewpoints either explain the Divine on the basis of other phenomena which they believe more fundamental or affirm a fact-value distinction which permits them to bifurcate the problem of interpreting religious phenomena.

Those who make this fact-value distinction either have an agnostic attitude toward religious phenomena or distinguish between objective,

FIGURE I

THE STRUCTURE OF THE ANALYSIS OF ALTERNATIVE PERSPECTIVES ON RELIGIOUS PHENOMENA AND RELIGIOUS INSTITUTIONS

I

NON-*SUI GENERIS* PERSPECTIVES BASED ON NON-THEISTIC ROOT PRESUPPOSITIONS

Phenomenological, related to an appeal to "experience" which does not incorporate a transcendent or depth dimension to reality

Atomistic or elemental, focused on underlying parts or factors which "explain" religious phenomena

Existential, focused on dynamics

Situational, focused on form

"Epiphenomenal" religious institution, explained by examining causal sequences and parts which constitute a whole

"Charismatic" religious institution, rooted in actions of charismatic religious leaders

"Societal" religious institution, rooted in social phenomena embedded in nature

FIGURE II

SUI GENERIS PERSPECTIVES, INVOLVING A
TRANSCENDENT OR DEPTH DIMENSION IN REALITY
OR SOME TYPE OF WORLD BEHIND THE WORLD

Types of God-World Relations Possible

God immanent in world

God transcendent of world

God immanent in and transcendent of the world

"Cultural" religious institution

"World denying" religious institution

"One-way" immanent-transcendent God-world relations

"Two-way" immanent-transcendent God-world relations

Special, unique, locus of revelation

General and special loci of revelation

General locus of revelation

Form accentuated secondarily . .to. . Form minimized secondarily

Form accentuated . . to . . Dynamics accentuated

Authentic religious institution; form is affirmed, but is not made absolute

Specific authentic religious institution . .to. . Dynamic and authentic amorphous religious institution

Specific . .to. authentic religious institution . . to . . Relatively more amorphous authentic religious institution

Authentic religious institution; form is affirmed, but is not made absolute

FIGURE III

ALTERNATIVE FACT-VALUE RELATIONS GUIDING ONE'S VIEW OF RELATIONS BETWEEN I AND II

Fact and Value Unrelated		Fact and Value Interrelated
Confessional studies	Scientific studies	Clear-cut distinctions between confessional and scientific studies untenable; may incorporate several perspectives in a single investigation
Sui generis perspectives on religious phenomena and religious institutions	Non-*sui generis* perspectives on religious phenomena and religious institutions	

theoretical, analytic studies of religious phenomena made by scientists and subjective, practical, confessional affirmations made by believers. Max Weber is one of the most distinguished proponents of the first approach; H. Richard Niebuhr, of the second.[3]

Social scientists who make this basic fact-value distinction may disagree about analytical methods used in studies of religious phenomena. Differences about whole-part, form-dynamic and linguistic symbol-human experience relations may develop between them. It is beyond the scope of this chapter to consider these issues, for the primary focus here is upon the consequences of alternative perspectives for the basic interpretation of religious institutions.

PHENOMENOLOGICAL PERSPECTIVES ON RELIGIOUS PHENOMENA

Protagonists of phenomenological perspectives on religious phenomena either do not concede the reality of a transcendent subject-object of religious devotion or a depth dimension in experience or else consider it beyond the bounds of scientific inquiry. They focus upon phenomena found in "concrete" experience, but do not think that some transcendent or immanent-transcendent Supreme Referee is needed to interpret religious experience.

Phenomenologists may emphasize either the dynamic or the formal side of experience. If they emphasize dynamics, they develop self-affirming or self-making views of religious phenomena. If they emphasize form, they develop theories focuses upon structures and entities embedded in man's experience but at least partially independent of it. In this discussion the former type is termed an "existential phenomenological perspective"; the latter, a "situational phenomenological perspective."

Existential Phenomenological Perspective

Those who entertain this perspective interpret experience from the observer's perspective. Because definitions in the sciences are "operational," a consensus among workers in a particular field is the basis for the validation of theory. In the human sciences, the importance of decision is accentuated, since man's self-affirming and self-making character is emphasized. Although protagonists are interested in studying the manifestations of what some purport to be responses to the Divine, they refrain from considering the nature of the Divine Himself. They juxtapose man-made conditioning dimensions, originally established by the willful decisions of elites and subsequently institutionalized in society, with the decisions of individual agents.

Situational Phenomenological Perspective

Protagonists of this perspective see religious phenomena embedded in man's relations with external entities which are natural, social, or both. Although they deny the *sui generis* character of the subject-object of religious devotion referred to by the verbal symbol "God," they do affirm an extra-human dimension in existence. Scientists who analyze this extra-human dimension are able to illumine the genuine basis for phenomena which other men term "religious."

Historical and Contemporary Importance of Phenomenological Perspectives

These two phenomenological perspectives have been of great historical importance in the social scientific study of religious phenomena. Max Weber used facets of the existential variant, and Emile Durkheim appealed to the situational variant when he located the ground of religion in society.[4] Because of their emphasis on dynamics, Protestant analysts have frequently been sympathetic with the existentialist perspective. Roman Catholic theorists, because of their stress on form, have often been more sympathetic with the situational viewpoint.[5]

Protestant scholars maintaining a fact-value disjunction have produced several significant empirical studies of religious phenomena which have incorporated both the transcendent-immanent God-world relation of the "one-way" type discussed below and a Weberian perspective on the social studies. Kenneth Underwood's *Protestant and Catholic*, Paul Harrison's *Authority and Power in the Free Church Tradition*, and Henry Clark's *The Church and Residential Desegregation* reflect this orientation.[6] All of them affirm the *sui generis* character of religious experience, and all of them incorporate normative dimensions in their analyses. At the same time, they separate empirical and normative material in their investigations.

W. Lloyd Warner employs a situational phenomenological perspective in *The Family of God*, but the purity of the perspective is compromised by his use of some psychoanalytic ideas to interpret religious phenomena.[7]

Because both the situational and the elemental or atomistic perspective discussed in the following sub-section interpret religious phenomena on the basis of other factors, the relation between them is tantalizingly close. From some points of view, it is impossible to distinguish these two perspectives.

ATOMISTIC OR ELEMENTAL PERSPECTIVES ON RELIGIOUS PHENOMENA

Protagonists of the atomistic or elemental perspective on the subject-object of religious experience look for some underlying elements or components on the basis of which they may explain religious experience. They attempt to understand God by referring to elements or components which they allege have produced men's ideas and/or feelings about Him. Freud's interpretation of God as the projection of a father figure is an example of this perspective.[8]

This perspective is closely related to the situational phenomenological perspective. The atomistic or elemental approach reduces religious phenomena to elemental factors or components which underlie and produce them; the situational phenomenological approach explains religious phenomena by referring to natural entities external to man. In either case, both sociological and psychological factors may be involved. Some analysts fuse these two prespectives. Charles Y. Glock, for example, employs a gratification-deprivation psychological balance in relation to social-institution configurations to explain the emergence of sects.[9]

THE CONTEMPORARY IMPORTANCE OF PHENOMENOLOGICAL
AND
ELEMENTAL PERSPECTIVES ON RELIGIOUS PHENOMENA

The authors of most contemporary studies of religious phenomena in the United States advance interpretations informed by one of the three perspectives just delineated or by some combination of them. Social scientists who affirm the fact-value disjunction usually do not develop the confessional side of this dichotomy.[10] Therefore, the interpretations of religious phenomena offered by workers such as Gordon Allport, Kingsley Davis, N. J. Demerath III, Erich Fromm, Charles Y. Glock, Thomas Hoult, Gerhard Lenski, Talcott Parsons, Guy Swanson, Glen Vernon, W. Lloyd Warner, and J. Milton Yinger differ in part from the interpretations advanced by those who affirm a subject-object of religious experience that is, in some sense, *sui generis*.[11] Because methodological and interpretive dimensions are intertwined in empirical studies, these interpretive perspectives are modified by some protagonists, but the broad distinction between writers who affirm the *sui generis* subject-object of religious experience and those who do not remains. The methodological decision to break a whole into constituent parts or to build a whole out of component parts frequently contributes to this "blurring." The very title of Gerhard Lenski's book, *The Religious Factor,* for example, highlights the pervasive contemporary methodological predilection among social scientists. A more detailed discussion of this matter can be found in Part Three.

Those informed by an ontological perspective insist on a supreme, transcendent dimension in reality. Such views are intertwined with alternative conceptualizations of God-world relations. These two related matters are considered in the following discussion of varieties of the fourth broad perspective on the interpretation of religious phenomena.

SUI GENERIS PERSPECTIVES ON RELIGIOUS PHENOMENA

Persons who affirm the *sui generis* character of religious phenomena are guided by their views of God-world relations. Three broad relations between God and the world are formally possible. God may be conceived as totally immanent in the world, as partially immanent in and partially transcendent of the world, or as totally transcendent of the world. This tripartite formulation of alternative God-world relations is based upon the formally possible relations between two entities—identity, contiguity, overlap, and independence.

Immanent God-World Relations

Protagonists who hold that God is totally immanent in the world necessarily reject a supreme and transcendent dimension in reality; therefore, this option becomes a variation of one of the two phenomenological options discussed above and is not considered further here.[12]

Transcendent God-World Relations

Proponents of the view that God is totally transcendent of the world must deny the reality of the world. They suggest its illusory character and develop various means to overcome the subject-object cleavage found in human experience. Since they seek absorption into an entity that is at once all and nothing, this view bears some relation to the view that God is totally immanent in the world.[13]

Immanent-Transcendent God-World Relations

The other alternative God-world relations represent variations of the immanent-transcendent God-world options.[14] Two sub-types are possible.

The first sub-type is a one-way immanent-transcendent God-world relation: a protagonist affirms God's action upon the world, but denies, explicitly or implicitly, the world's action upon God. Most major Christian theologians have held some form of this alternative. A protagonist's view of the extent to which and the manner in which man experiences the immanent character of God in the world depends upon the protagonist's conception of sin and upon his understanding of the relation between form and dynamics in God.

The second sub-type is a two-way immanent-transcendent God-world relation. Proponents hold that just as the Divine Life contributes to the life of the world, so the world contributes to the Divine Life. Because of the reciprocity of the God-world relation, both form and dynamics are included. No unique locus of God's revelation to man is possible. There is, therefore, only one variety of this sub-type.

ONE-WAY IMMANENT-TRANSCENDENT GOD-WORLD RELATIONS

Proponents of the one-way immanent-transcendent God-world relation entertain different views of the way in which man becomes aware of the Divine. As noted earlier, these differences are related to the theologian's view of man's relation to the Divine and to his conception of the relation of form and dynamics in the Divine. One may hold that man's awareness of the Divine is due unequivocally to the Divine initiative in a unique and concrete locus, that it is due in part to man's universal experience and in part to the Divine initiative in a unique and concrete locus, or that it is due to man's universal experience of the Divine. These alternatives are discussed sequentially.

Unique and concrete locus of the Divine revelation. Those who entertain this view hold that man's apprehension of the Divine nature can occur only because God, by His initiative in the height of His freedom, revealed Himself to man. This emphasis upon a dynamic or transdynamic "will" in the Divine nature focuses God's revelation upon an event or a series of events, so His self-revelation must have a unique and concrete locus.

In the Christian tradition, this view has frequently been associated with a doctrine of original sin or total depravity and man's resultant loss of his original perfectly harmonious relation with the Divine. This original relation may be located spatially and temporally, internally and psychologically, or both. The unique locus is customarily centered in Jesus Christ and attested to in the Christian Bible and/or the Christian Church. The tradition, then, provides the dimension of form, and the believer's personal encounter with the Divine through the work of the Holy Spirit is set in relation to his tradition. Karl Barth and H. Richard Niebuhr illustrate this point of view.[15]

There is no *a priori* reason why the locus of revelation must be confined to a particular tradition; some theologians generalize it to include any locus. Harvey Cox reflects this perspective, which can also be seen as a variety of the third sub-type noted later.[16] Although he universalizes the locus of God's revelation, Cox minimizes the significance of form. Having rejected metaphysics and ontology, Cox dissociates himself from Paul Tillich, with whom he does have other affinities.

So-called Biblical fundamentalists accentuate the dimension of form, so the precise shape of the Scriptures becomes very important. Theologians such as Barth and H. Richard Niebuhr relate the Scriptures to man's inner history so that it is not tied to special cosmological and biological theories, but fundamentalists seek to universalize the cosmological and biological details found in the Christian Scriptures.

General and special loci of the Divine revelation. Those who affirm man's general and universal participation in the form or *logos* facet of the Divine Life have more equivocal views of the way in which man apprehends the Divine. Although they hold that God's ultimate character can be discerned only in a concrete and special locus, they think that man may attain some understanding of God through the universal experience of mankind.

In the Christian tradition, the concrete locus is the Christ event, to which witness is borne in the Church, in the Christian Bible, and in the personal experience of the believer. Roman Catholic theologians have characteristically placed a greater emphasis upon form than Protestant theologians who generally stress dynamics. Thus, Catholic protagonists of this view of immanent-transcendent God-world relations advance the familiar levels of being and the natural-supernatural distinctions of the Roman Catholic tradition.[17] Protestant theologians who uphold the dominance of dynamics in the Divine blur the distinctions between the levels of being and the facets of God's nature.[18]

General locus of the Divine revelation. Although most Protestant and Catholic theologians have, in some fashion, focused God's revelation of Himself on a particular historical locus, there is no *a priori* reason to limit the revelation to a particular historical tradition or institution. Rudolph Otto reflects this view, for he emphasizes the universal experience of the Divine among men.[19]

Although no major contemporary Christian theologian emphasizes unequivocally the dimension of form in the Divine nature, this perspective has been reflected in the thinking of some eighteenth-and nineteenth-century deists, who found God reflected in the perfect workings of nature.

TWO-WAY IMMANENT-TRANSCENDENT GOD-WORLD RELATIONS

The final God-world relation is one in which protagonists discern a reciprocal relation between God and the world. Each contributes to the life of the other. Because of this reciprocal relation, any human experience possesses, in principle, the capacity to illumine the nature of things. God functions in the universe as the locus of potentiality, as the mediator of experience, as the lure for feeling, and as the ultimate receptor of all that has become in the world.[20]

As noted previously, one's view of religious institutions is inextricably related to these alternative perspectives on the grounds for religious phenomena. If a protagonist affirms that religious experience is *sui generis*, his view of the institution related to that experience is shaped by the type of God-world relation which he envisions.

Because of the multiplicity of *sui generis* and non-*sui generis* perspectives, two investigators may disagree fundamentally about the nature and type of institution which should be identified and studied as a "religious" institution. The following section explores the alternative perspectives on the religious institution which emerge from the various basic grounds for religious phenomena just described.

Alternative Perspectives on the Nature of Religious Institutions

Protagonists of phenomenological, elemental, and transcendent perspectives differ in their fundamental understanding of the religious institution. Institutions which some people consider religious will not be so considered by others. Although one may empathize with the interpretations of the elites who shape the internal understanding of various religious institutions by sympathetically examining their positions, these basic differences in perspective will persist. Every social scientist and every religious professional, by omission or commission, must decide on the adequacy of his own informing perspective. Because methodological and substantive dimensions are intertwined, it is frequently possible to sort them out only by distorting a writer's views to some extent. Some readers may think this categorization produces such distortions. Nevertheless, the broad distinction between *sui generis* and non-*sui generis* interpretations of religious phenomena still stands.

PHENOMENOLOGICAL PERSPECTIVES ON RELIGIOUS INSTITUTIONS

Protagonists of the two phenomenological perspectives on religious phenomena do not assign any unique character to the religious institution. Proponents of the existential or self-affirming phenomenological perspective do not attempt to explain religious institutions on the basis of other phenomena; proponents of the situational phenomenological interpretation set religious institutions in relation to something embedded in nature.

Existential Phenomenological Perspective

Proponents of this perspective hold that all voluntary associations, including religious institutions, are ultimately rooted in the decisions of individual actors. The analyst may appeal to habit or sentiment to explain some aspects of human involvement in religious institutions, but the ultimate referee is the individual's self-decision. For example, Max Weber's continued interest in charismatic religious leaders and in the importance of religious ideas and values in shaping human behavior may be interpreted in relation to his view of the importance of the human will in the development of religious institutions.[21] The special power of the charismatic religious leader contributes to the peculiar character of religious institutions.

Situational Phenomenological Perspective

Although analysts informed by this perspective do not interpret religious institutions on *sui generis* grounds, they do look beyond individual self-decision. Emile Durkheim, for example, roots the institution which he calls the church in society. Society is natural but possesses a life of its own. It is both internal and external to man, so it both attracts and has power over him, The sacred or set apart character of the religious institution is grounded in society, which the participant is actually worshiping, though he thinks he is worshiping the Divine.[22] W. Lloyd Warner employs such an interpretation of religious institutions in *Democracy in Jonesville* and *The Family of God*, though the latter volume is complicated by his appeal to some psychoanalytic notions.[23]

ATOMISTIC OR ELEMENTAL PERSPECTIVES ON
RELIGIOUS INSTITUTIONS

Analysts who seek to discern casual factors behind religious institutions focus their analyses on component parts which give rise to them. Some of Karl Marx's and Sigmund Freud's writings represent classic illustrations. Though no major contemporary empirical study of religious institutions in the United States unequivocally interprets religious instutitions epiphenomenonally, workers informed by Durkheimian views are tantalizingly close to such an interpretation.

Many contemporary social scientists in the United States, nevertheless, do seek to explain a whole by breaking it into component parts. This approach results in an "impure" atomistic interpretation of religious institutions. The ambiguity of this approach is reflected in Gerhard Lenski's *The Religious Factor.*[24] Lenski attempts to refute proponents of casual determinism and religious epiphenomenonalism by showing that one's affiliation with religious institutions does affect one's beliefs, attitudes and behavior, but his analytical method assumes that a whole is made up of the sum of its parts. This presupposition permits him to apply statistical controls and various time-sequence tests to component parts to assess in a relatively precise manner the contribution which religious institutions make to their adherents' beliefs, attitudes and behavior. It leads him in the direction of multi-casual determinism and encourages him to focus strongly on the casual past.[25]

SUI GENERIS PERSPECTIVES ON RELIGIOUS INSTITUTIONS

Those who affirm that religious institutions are ultimately grounded in man's response to a subject-object Who is, at least in some sense, supreme and *sui generis* must include a discussion of Him and His relation to the religious institution in their analyses of such institutions. The shape of alternative *sui generis* perspectives on religious institutions is directly related to the alternative God-world relations discussed in the preceding section. This sub-section outlines the *sui generis* understandings of religious institutions which emerge from the God-world relations delineated there.

Immanent God-World Relations and Sui Generis *Perspectives on Religious Institutions*

Those who hold that God is totally immanent in the world do not assign any unique character to the religious institution. Because they advance no transcendent referee, proponents of this view may suggest that the institution which embodies and/or sanctifies the highest values or ideals of a given culture or sub-culture is a religious institution. Although some liberal American Protestants in the early part of this century supported this view, there are no major contemporary theological proponents of this interpretation of the religious institution. However, many critics of "culture" religion, informed by a transcendent-immanent God-world perspective, have suggested that religious institutions in the United States have become mere sanctifiers of man-made cultural values and have criticized the leaders and members of such instutitions for their idolatrous propensities.[26]

Transcendent God-World Relations and Sui Generis *Perspectives on Religious Institutions*

Proponents of a totally transcendent God cannot establish any special grounds for the religious institution. This view tends to undercut any positive basis for a religious institution; the amorphous character of Hindu religious institutions is typical. Persons persuaded of the Divine's transcendent character may form a group who develop a variety of practices to negate the world and to affirm its illusory character; but they usually display highly individualistic practices and tendencies.

Immanent-Transcendent God-World Relations and Sui Generis
Perspectives on Religious Institutions

Although their interpretations are conditioned by the type of God-world relation which they presuppose, proponents of all the immanent-transcendent God-world relations ascribe a *sui generis* character to the religious institution. Some will be able to delineate a religious institution quite sharply; others will find the differences between a religious institution and other forms of human association much more diffuse. Although they may acknowledge the actions of charismatic leaders, forms embedded in culture and the social order, and conditioning dimensions incorporated in the casual past, proponents of this perspective will not be satisfied with interpretations which rely exclusively on such explanations.

ONE-WAY IMMANENT-TRANSCENDENT GOD-WORLD RELATIONS
AND *Sui Generis* PERSPECTIVES ON RELIGIOUS
INSTITUTIONS

Unique and concrete locus of the Divine revelation and sui generis perspectives on religious institutions. Those who hold that God is radically "other" insist that man encounters the Divine only through His self-revelation in an unique way. This observation is the only formal one that can be made, for man may discern the locus of revelation only experientially and concretely. The locus most generally affirmed by Christian theologians is one's personal experience set in relation to Jesus Christ, the Scriptures, the Christian Church, and the work of the Holy Spirit.

A protagonist's view of the form of the Church may range from specific to general. The former view is reflected by those who affirm that the Christian Church is a God-given institution for the salvation of mankind and is usually (or always) identified by the Bible, the Sacraments, and the ministry.[27] The latter view is reflected by those who hold that the concrete experience of God's sacrificing love may be encountered in any locus, which then becomes the Church.[28]

A sociologist seeking to study the Church, understood from this latter point of view, is going to have a difficult time for the form is too dynamic to be isolated for study. As noted earlier, protagonists of this point of view insist upon the unequivocal dominance of dynamics in the man-God encounter, but they universalize the locus of revelation. In this sense, they agree with those who affirm a general locus for the Divine revelation.

General and special loci of the Divine revelation and sui generis perspectives on religious institutions. Proponents of this perspective incorporate both dynamics and form in their interpretation of the Divine nature and His relation to the world. The Roman Catholic version accentuates form, but relates it to the Church's special role as the harbinger of truth and the custodian of morality. This combination of formal universality and concrete specificity results in appeal both to general and special revelation.[29] The stress on form is reflected in the type of casuistry developed, the emphasis given to the Sacraments, the priest's mediating role, and, indirectly, the hierarchical structure of the Roman Catholic Church.

Protestant variants of this perspective are less clear about the nature of the Church, the form of morality, the role of the religious professional, ideal belief systems, and the form or substance of the practice of worship. Reinhold Niebuhr, for example, holds that man's understanding of God as Creator and Judge are part of the general experience of mankind, but that man's awareness of God as Redemptive Love is made clear only in the special revelation of Jesus Christ.[30] Niebuhr thinks that the peculiar locus of this awareness is man's experience set in relation to the Biblical witness, but he also advances the notion of a "hidden Christ" to transcend the special history of the segment of mankind which knows Christ "after the flesh." Religious institutions and the Christian Church, then, are not so readily identifiable as in Roman Catholicism and in some other Protestant understandings. However, the Scriptures and the tradition do permit a provisional delineation of the Christian Church.

General locus of the Divine revelation and sui generis perspectives on religious institutions. Although a proponent of the one-way immanent-transcendent God-world relation may universalize the locus of God's revelation, he may still focus it upon a concrete encounter. In this case, he may affirm the provisional but not the absolute value of a particular religious institution or a particular form and substance of worship.

Rudolph Otto, for example, employs philosophic rather than Biblical language in his religious studies, refuses to ascribe any absolute significance to particular forms of worship, and sees the universal manifestation of the Divine nature in man's encounter with religious meaning. At the same time, he affirms the Church as a bearer of religious meaning.[31] The appropriateness of given forms of sacrament, worship or church is intertwined with the nature of the socio-culture context in which they are set.

TWO-WAY IMMANENT-TRANSCENDENT GOD-WORLD RELATIONS
AND *Sui Generis* PERSPECTIVES ON RELIGIOUS INSTITUTIONS

Proponents of this perspective presuppose necessary reciprocity and mutual implication between God and the world. Although those informed by this perspective hold that in principle no experience of mankind is incapable of illumining the nature of the Divine, they readily acknowledge that certain experiences are more evocative of religious experience than others. Similarly, some people may find the cluster of feeling and meaning associated with a particular religious institution illumines that harmony of harmonies which is part of God's nature; others may find the same institution a hindrance to their quest for religious and theological understanding. This plurality necessitates some appreciation of a multiplicity of cognitive and emotive religious forms and practices.

Proponents of this perspective ground the religious institution in the universal religious experience of mankind. The religious institution bears special witness to God's primordial nature, His once-for-all envisagement of all potentiality, but it should also affirm His total nature. On principle those informed by this perspective ascribe no unique categorical significance to a particular religious institution, form of worship, or sacred Scripture; in fact, they may affirm the matrix of feeling and meaning associated with particular patterns and may make judgments about the appropriateness of various styles of worship and theological understanding.[32]

No unequivocal identification of a religious institution is possible. A variety of religious symbols and practices evoke varied responses among men. Nevertheless, religious institutions may be provisionally identified by patterns of worship, religious instruction and social interaction.

The Religious Professional and the Religious Institution

The religious professional must make a normative theological judgment about the nature and character of the religious institution, for the locus and style of his ministry is inextricably related to his implicit or explicit judgments about this matter. The three broad immanent-transcendent God-world relations lead to different conceptions of the nature of the ministry.

Those who hold that God is totally immanent in the world or totally transcendent of the world can ascribe no categorically distinctive role to the religious professional. The religious professional is a teacher who illumines either the nature of an immanent good or the illusory character of the world.

Theologians who think that the radical otherness of God in human experience is due to man's inordinate self-centeredness and the character of the Divine-human encounter develop an understanding of the religious professional which is informed by the locus and nature of God's revelation of Himself to sinful man.[33]

Protestant theologians have frequently emphasized the peculiar role of the religious professional in the preaching of the Word, Jesus Christ, through Biblical exegesis and in the administration of the Sacraments. God may reveal Himself to the worshiper in the preaching of the religious professional and in his reception of the Sacraments, but almost all Protestant theologians deny the religious professional any special mediating role between man and God.

Although many Protestant theologians who accentuate this theo-volitional character of Divine revelation emphasize the vehicle through which the revelation is made, they refuse to make it absolute. Other theologians, however, may accentuate the significance of the vehicle through which the revelation takes place; Biblical fundamentalists represent this approach. In either case, a proponent may be fairly clear about the nature of the religious professional's role, for his primary task is to preach the Word through Biblical exegesis and to administer the Sacraments.

Theologians who generalize the locus of God's dynamic action may deny that the religious professional possesses a special and unique role or that the religious institution called the Christian Church can be identified by any formal characteristics. Since proponents of this extremely dynamic view of the religious institution can establish no unique role for the religious professional, religious professionals influenced by this view are naturally uncertain about their roles. It is possible that persons who affirm this perspective may foster the emergence of some new form of sectarian, voluntary religious institution.

Christian theologians who believe that man possesses a limited general awareness of God's nature discern a special locus of His revelation in the "Holy Community" which is established by His revelation of His full nature. The religious professional is a witness and mediator of symbols significant to this community and to His revelation.

Both Protestant and Catholic theologians may accept some notion of "general" revelation, but they may also emphasize the special character of the Church. The variations in interpretation among Protestant theologians are comparable to the ones just considered, so the role of the religious professional may be more or less clear. Roman Catholic theologians have usually ascribed special mediating and sacerdotal functions to the religious professional, so his role in the Church and in God's plan of salvation is relatively very clear.

Theologians who universalize man's experience of the Trinity can discern God's revelation potentially in any locus; the religious professional mediates the signs and symbols which are significant bearers of meaning and revelation to a particular group. Proponents of this view hold that the form of the religious institution is provisional. However, since they affirm the need for some form and a belief system to sustain the religious institution, the religious professional does have some special responsibilities.

Theologians who affirm the two-way immanent-transcendent God-world relation maintain that any locus possesses the potential to illumine God's character. This view ascribes a role to the religious professional which is similar to the view held by protagonists of the one-way immanent-transcendent God-world relation noted in the preceding paragraph. Although this interpretation precludes any unequivocally clear delineation of the religious institution, some type of religious institution can be discerned in all societies. In contrast to some variants of the one-way immanent-transcendent type of God-world relations, this two-wayview affirms the universal religiousness of mankind and expects religious institutions which bear special witness to the Divine presence to emerge in all cultures at all times. Proponents of this view emphasize the teaching role of the religious professional, the interpreter and evoker of the meaning which his historical community bears.

As noted earlier, those who maintain the interrelatedness of fact and value cannot be satisfied with a mere analysis of alternative viewpoints on a given topic. Such analysis is necessary but not sufficient. It must be supplemented in appropriate contexts with a constructive interpretation of the issues under discussion. The final section of this chapter is devoted to one such constructive interpretation.

An Interpretation of the Nature of the Church and the Role of the Religious Professional in Contemporary American Society

In the United States laymen in all the major denominations expect the religious professional in a local church to exercise an adjustive and integrative role; they hold cognitive, prophetic, and administrative capacities in relatively low esteem.[34] Although this leadership role does require a dominantly affective and diffuse role definition, the religious professional's response to these lay expectations depends upon his own vision of his task. Every genuine religious professional must determine which informing cognitive structures will shape his ministry.

A religious professional in a local church must perform ceremonial activities related to birth, puberty, marriage, and death, for these rites of passage are rooted in the "physical" side of man and are elicited by age grading, sexual differentiation, and the contingencies of existence. He must also give a measure of sanctification to the special ceremonial occasions of great cognitive-emotive symbolic significance to the members of a society. In contemporary American society, Memorial Day, Independence Day, Veteran's Day and Thanksgiving possess such symbolic significance.[35]

Because it is held here that monogamy is the best possible form of family organization, that a modified enterprise system is a viable form of economic organization, that public education is a necessary base for the lure for excellence and a measure of equality, that cultural pluralism is desirable, that a federated type of democracy is the best possible form of large-scale political organization, that religious pluralism is desirable and that religious freedom is normative for human beings, a religious professional's basic stance toward a society in which these forms are institutionalized and are functioning in a tolerably adequate manner should be ambiguously positive.[36] Therefore, a religious professional in American society may readily perform rites of passage, offer a degree of sanctification to great national symbolic events, and give qualified support to the existing forms of social organization in American society.

The Christian tradition, which has had some influence on everyone in the West, has made an ambiguously positive contribution to the life of civilized mankind, but the view that the Christian Church is grounded on a categorically unique base must be questioned. Religious institutions are based on man's intuitive awareness of a vision of perfection and a lure for harmony and intensity of feeling which are part of the Divine nature. These characteristics of God's nature give the religious institution a distinctive place among human institutions and provide the religious professional with a special role as a leader of public worship, as an educator, and as the director of an institution which sustains these activities and fosters social relations among its members. They do not permit one such institution or tradition to insist on its singular priority among religious institutions because of God's special revelation to mankind through it or its symbols.

God functions in the universe as the locus of potentiality, as a lure for feeling, as a mediator of experience, and as the receptor of all that the world has to offer to Him. The fundamental character of religious experience, understood as the supreme harmonious fusion of conceptual and physical feelings in man's experience as he becomes aware of the Divine presence, and the significance of reason in interpreting that experience highlight the importance of worship and teaching in the church. Man's participation in a particular religious tradition provides the sensitive religious professional with a storehouse of evocative symbols which he may use to reinforce and nurture religious experience, while the manifestation of God's activity in all experience permits him to draw on contemporary experience to demonstrate the nature of the Divine.

The social character of existence and man's need for intensity and richness of experience allow for an ambiguously positive interpretation of the social functions of many contemporary American religious institutions. Although many activities in such institutions are superficial, they do sustain a measure of human sociability.[37]

The social nature of life and the lure for harmony contribute to man's desire to serve in the world, but a note of caution must be raised about the kind of service sponsored directly by religious institutions. They may sponsor programs which provide direct service to persons in need, but they should exercise the greatest reserve about direct sponsorship or support of particular political-economic programs or special political-economic causes because of the conflict between love, principles of justice, and rules and regulations of justice.

Despite this note of caution, theologians who believe a federated democracy the best attainable form of political organization may encourage members of religious institutions to support this form of political organization in areas where it has been institutionalized. Religious professionals may foster contexts in which the theological implications of political and economic issues can be explored, may express the religious institution's concern about public issues at the level of principles of justice, and may encourage members of their institutions to participate as responsible citizens in the body politic.

These admonitions and affirmations are based on the contrast between an ultimate harmony of harmonies or a vision of perfection discerned in potentiality and the ambiguity inherent in all actuality. The former dimension of experience is embedded in God's primordial nature, for God's once-for-all envisagement of all potentiality constitutes the harmony and lure for intensity of feeling which is at the base of things. The latter dimension of experience is embedded in the finite character of all actualization, for the realization of some possibilities necessarily excludes the realization of other possibilities. Men's inability to harmonize completely the principle of equality appropriate to form with the principle of self-determination informed by excellence reflects this "isness-oughtness" contrast.[38]

Although men's experience of a transcendent or primordial vision provides the basis for the religious institution, they perennially appropriate differentially both the cognitive and trans-cognitive dimensions of religious experience. Any religious professional who can accept this fundamental condition and who can make an ambiguously positive theological interpretation of the basic structures of American society should have no trouble serving in a wide range of religious institutions in the United States.[39] The religious professional should not ignore creative, innovative and prophetic activities, but in the United States his primary aims should be adjustive and integrative.

Discussions of the relations of religious institutions to American society and culture should begin by affirming, with certain qualifications, both institutional religious life in the United States and the basic structures of American society. Although sectarians and classical Lutherans, for different reasons, may criticize existing structures and practices among religious institutions in the United States, all religious professionals who can see a positive relation between the dominant social structures of the United States and theological understanding may begin their work with a more affirmative view. Because of the inevitability of some disharmony in the world and the numerous negative aspects of American life, they clearly must reject utopian views. Nevertheless, they may undertake an ambiguously positive interpretation of the relation between religious institutions and American culture.

The true religious professional must be motivated by a sense of cause which he can maintain with integrity. He may be guided in his development of a sense of cause by one of the theological perspectives discussed earlier or by the one advanced here.

However, a religious professional with extensive cognitive understanding and commitment may still be inadequate unless he possesses certain inner qualities. In addition to his commitment to a cause, the authentic religious professional must also maintain a sense of proportion and possess a sense of responsibility.[40] A sense of proportion is essential since he must make judgments about the relative importance of various activities and events in his personal life, in the life of a religious institution or other corporate group to which he is related professionally, and in the life of society. He must wisely allocate his time and efforts among the varied demands upon him.

The religious professional must attempt to foresee the consequences of his activities as the leader of a congregation and must be prepared to bear the consequences for his actions. If the religious professional is to exercise this sense of responsibility, he must understand the fundamental processes which shape individual and group life. Social scientific studies may help him to develop this understanding, for they may enhance his grasp of the dynamics of group life. Developing "feed-back" procedures may help him to be sensitive to the needs and expectations of his congregation and to evaluate the differential impact of various programs initiated in the congregation.

The genuine religious professional is one in whom a sense of service to a cause, a sense of proportion, and a sense of responsibility function harmoniously. Such a person may reasonably expect to make an ambiguously positive contribution to the personal and corporate life of mankind.

Chapter XII

Love, Justice and Forms of Social Organization

Since love is the linguistic symbol which most adequately describes the Divine, the relations between God and the world noted in the preceding chapter focus upon the central topic of this chapter. Because of the common subject-object and an ordering typology based on the same general notions, the formulations here parallel the ones developed in Chapter XI. However, further dimensions are introduced here.

The following section considers the nature of the Trinity. The second and third sections discuss the relation of love and justice from transcendent triadic perspectives. The final section presents a constructive interpretation of the issues considered in the earlier sections. Although visual linguistic symbols encourage a sequential discussion and the separation of a whole into component parts, the sections of this chapter are, in fact, interrelated; in the categorical portions of this discussion the starting point is arbitrary.

Proponents of any of the immanent-transcendent God-world relations described in Chapter XI are usually trinitarians; they almost invariably discern in experience some formal, rational or patterned component, a basic creative urge or power, and a lure for the harmonious unification of form and power.

The formal or rational component is exhibited, for example, in the *logos* dimension of classical Christian trinitarian formulations, in the forms of Plato, in the Being of Paul Tillich, and in the eternal objects of Alfred N. Whitehead. The notion of a basic creative urge or power appears in the idea of the Father in classical Christian trinitarian formulations, in the Good in Plato, in power related to the ground of Being in Tillich, and in the category of creativity in Whitehead. The lure toward the unification of these components is expressed by the notion of the Holy Spirit in classical Christian trinitarian formulations, probably of the Good in relation to a series of lesser gods and other events in Plato, of love as *agape* in Tillich, and of the functioning of God, taking His primordial and consequent natures in their proper unity, in Whitehead.

Christians who deny that man's reason participates in Being or in something analogous to Being locate the dimension of form in the concreteness of God's revelation in the Word, Jesus Christ, and in the context in which one finds oneself; having unqualifiedly espoused the ultimacy of the dynamic, they must turn to a context to get the dimensions of form or to get the analogs of what, from other perspectives, are termed dimensions of form.

One may entertain either a process view of the becoming of an entity or a substance view of the being of an entity. These alternative perspectives condition one's understanding of perfection and of the meaning which one ascribes to the term "love." In substance alternatives, love is manifest supremely in God's unification of Himself with Himself. In process alternatives, love is realized supremely in God's sensitive response to the world and in His everlasting reception into Himself of all that the world has to offer.

If a theologian contrasts a single type of perfection (an ultimate harmony of harmonies, an ultimate peace of peace, a dynamic pattern of perfect love, or an ultimate wisdom of wisdom) with the actual situation, he is probably informed by a substance view of the created entity. Augustine makes this contrast more or less implicitly; Thomas Aquinas makes it explicitly. If a theologian denies a single type of perfection, he is probably guided by a process and relational view of the nature of the created entity. Plato hints at such a view; A. N. Whitehead and Charles Hartshorne explicitly develop this view.

Although the intrinsic interrelatedness of the components means that the contrasts are equivocal, the difference between these two alternatives may be interpreted in relation to the components of the Trinity. Classical Christian trinitarian formulations emphasize the Father or the Son; process formulations stress the Holy Spirit. Classical Protestant thought emphasizes the Father and sets the Son and the Holy Spirit in relation to Him, while classical Roman Catholic thought emphasizes the Son and sets the Father and the Holy Spirit in relation to Him. The dimension of dynamics, therefore, receives greater emphasis in classical Protestantism;

the dimension of form, greater emphasis in classical Roman Catholicism.

In process thought the Divine lure for harmony and for intensity of feeling accentuates the presence of the Holy Spirit in the emergence of an actual entity. God's supreme sensitivity to the world and His appropriation into the Divine Life of all actual entities which have become represent love par excellence.

Although these differing emphases affect the interpretations which they offer, those who affirm this triadic view employ a harmony-lack of harmony contrast to interpret the Good and its relation to the world. Their view of the God-world relation conditions the meaning which they ascribe to the term "ultimate harmony."

In spite of their disagreements about the means by which man becomes aware of the Divine, proponents of the one-way immanent-transcendent God-world relation contrast the perfect goodness of the Divine with the imperfection of the world. Classical theologians who assumed God's goodness, omniscience, and omnipotence had to undertake tortuous explanations of the disharmony manifestly evident in the created world. Augustine, for example, combined the idea of the sinfulness of man's will —his inordinate self-centeredness which disrupted the harmony of creation—with a doctrine of predestination to maintain God's goodness, omniscience, and omnipotence and, at the same time, to explain the presence of disharmony in human experience. Modern Protestant theologians have frequently used the Kantian distinctions between pure and practical reason to reformulate the cosmological facet of the question which Augustine considered and to focus the discussion on man's inner experience of a harmony-disharmony contrast.

Proponents of the two-way immanent-transcendent God-world relation maintain that the intuition of perfection is based upon man's apprehension of a part of the Divine nature, but they deny that the term "ultimate harmony" implies either an ultimate perfection or a God who is perfect in all ways. The attempt to identify this vision of perfection unqualifiedly with God or to seek its unqualified realization in the world is an error, they suggest, for the vision is real in potentiality but deficient in actuality. They hold that finitude, ignorance, and the freedom of creatures combine to make the presence of some evil in the world inevitable.

Justice is most closely related to the element of form in the form-power-unification triad, but thorough-going trinitarians who universalize these relations can move readily from one component to another.[1] The relation which one posits between love and justice reflects his understanding of God-world relations. These relations are examined typologically and constructively in the following two sections.

Love and the Principles of Justice

From triadic transcendent perspectives, "love," regardless of the epistemological option to which one appeals to establish the basis upon which man is informed by it, suggests the experience of harmony. Love unifies form and power, so, in this sense, it is transrational.

Justice, in contrast, focuses upon form, so rational considerations are dominant. One searches for principles which can guide one's decisions in corporate and personal life. The principles which emerge are dueness, based upon the form facet of the form-power-unification triad; freedom, based upon power; and order, based upon unification.

The question of dueness opens to the problem of equality, for the nature of one's due depends upon the way in which one is compared to others. At the most elemental level, equality is limited by natural forms. In the human realm, age and sex represent such natural limitations on the principle of equality. Ideally, equality appropriate to form is one of the principles of justice.

The harmonious contribution of the parts to a whole reflects the ideal ordering of dueness and freedom in some classical formulations guided by triadic views. For example, in Books II-IV of *The Republic* Plato explores the perfect harmony that would exist in the ideal state if each contributed according to his capacity and each received according to his due. In Books XI-XIV of *The City of God* Augustine discusses a paradise before the Fall in which a perfect harmony of life with life was manifest because man adhered to the Divine will.

Freedom as a principle of justice is rooted in the power dimension of the triad and in a transcendent creativity. Because of the relation of the elements in the triad, the freedom which serves as a principle of justice is a qualified self-determination. Such freedom may be termed self-determination informed by excellence.

Those who envision a single type of perfection hold that in the ideal world every one would be truly free because their choices would be in accord with the Divine will so that perfect harmony of life with life would be manifest. They attribute man's lack of true freedom to finitude, ignorance and/or sin.

Others reject the idea of a single type of perfection and envision a multiplicity of "perfections," each more or less relevant to its environment, which are awaiting realization in the evolution of the cosmos. They hold that disharmonious dimensions in the world are inevitable and see no need to appeal to the notions of the Fall and original sin to explain the emergence of disharmonious dimensions in experience because finitude, ignorance and freedom sufficiently account for man's experience of disharmony.

Proponents of some triadic transcendental options vigorously affirm God's unqualified freedom and power over the world and develop doctrines of predestination to hold together various facets of the theological schema. Augustine develops such a view as he elaborates his ideas of creation *ex nihilo* and of God's pre-ordained plan of salvation in *The City of God*.

Proponents of a process view suggest that the view of love inherent in such formulations is in error. They maintain that sensitive responses and lures toward harmony are embodied in the idea of love and hold that freedom, understood as man's *sui generis* response to data offered to him, is undermined by views which uphold God's unqualified omnipotence and omniscience. Because the lure toward harmony and the intensification of feeling are a part of man's experience, there are degrees of freedom in human life. Man is freer when his freedom is informed by the lure of excellence.

The final principle of justice involves the harmonious ordering of equality appropriate to form with freedom informed by excellence. Since these two principles are not perfectly compatible, some lack of order (disharmony) is inevitable. Therefore, protagonists affirming the same formal principles may disagree about the appropriate balance between freedom and equality and about the nature of one's due in a given context.

Some proponents of triadic perspectives will argue that the delineation of the principles of justice in this section are too formal and universal. It is true that this formulation favors the third one-way immanent-transcendent God-world relation and the two-way immanent-transcendent God-world relation described in Chapter XI, but it is impossible to develop absolutely neutral categories of analysis. Although some protagonists will also be dissatisfied with the typology of alternative love-justice relations developed in the following section, the discussion of these relations is guided by general geometric notions and is thus more neutral. The typology may illustrate the power of alternative views and help one to empathize with alternative perspectives.

A Typology of Love-Justice Relations

Three broad types of love-justice relations may be conceived formally. This typology, based on the notions of independence, contiguity, overlap, and identity, encompasses the most general relations between two entities.

First, a relation in which the spheres of love and justice are separated from each other is termed a Type I relation. Second, a relation in which the two spheres interrelate so that love and justice overlap or are contiguous is termed a Type II relation. Third, a relation in which love and justice coalesce so that one notion is subsumed by the other is termed a Type III relation.[2]

Two varieties of Types I and III and three varieties of Type II love-justice relations are possible. Even though the nature of the principles of justice varies with the type of love-justice relation which one maintains, seven relatively distinct relations are discernible between love and justice.

This discussion relates the various types to historical manifestations in the Christian tradition. However, the unique contingencies of history never coincide precisely with formal categorizations, so none of the cited traditions or figures will perfectly reflect the formal type. Historians interested in the unique and the particular will have no difficulty finding exceptions to the broad patterns. Nevertheless, the general configurations noted in this section are discernible in historical patterns and in the writings of persons in the several traditions.

Although social structures and personalities condition the shape of cognitive structures, the power of alternative understandings and man's freedom to decide what he is to be are the fundamental bases for variation within an historical tradition. Despite the "lure toward coherence" between cognitive structures, social structures, and personality characteristics, man's inner experience and thought forms are not unequivocally dependent upon external cultural, social, and psychological factors.

Both subtypes of Type I love-justice relations maintain the separation of the two spheres. Protagonists of Type I-A see a sharp disjunction between the experience of perfection, or love, and justice. Christian theologians advancing this view also hold that man has lost awareness of the Divine presence. Therefore, the discussion is frequently set in the context of gospel and law rather than in the context of love and justice to symbolize the importance of the Divine initiative in the restoration of man's awareness of his relation to God.

Martin Luther, for example, holds that the principalities and powers in the world are the consequence of sin. The gospel cannot be manifest directly in the political order, so a "strange" relation exists between gospel and law. Because of sin, men are subject to the political order, which they should endure. If a political order is relatively good, men are to thank God for His generosity; if relatively bad, men are being punished by God for their sins. Luther accentuates the principles of order and form in the world: the main function of the political realm is to maintain "order." His "orders of creation" leads to a hierarchical concept of the social order. The dominance of form and other results in a kind of quietism symbolized by the ideas that man should work "in" a vocation and that he should, in most cases, "obey" the magistrate.

Luther sets justice, seen indirectly in the orders of creation, outside of perfection and only partially rationalizes it. He sets equality in the context of a hierarchy and usually subordinates freedom to form and order. Love can be more clearly manifest in the family and in the church than anywhere else, but man's sinfulness limits the likelihood of a transformation of society.

Proponents of Type I-B love-justice relations reject the world and the structures of justice in the world. They advocate a radical withdrawal from the principalities and powers of the world and the establishment of a setting in which the harmony of life with life among the redeemed may be most fully realized. Menno Simons, for example, urged the group which later bore the name "Mennonites" to dissociate from the world.

Few proponents of this option systematically explore the relations between love and justice. The degree of rationalization which systematic considerations presuppose tends to undercut this option, since the problem of love-justice relations emerges because of one's awareness of some persistent contrast between them.

Proponents of Type I-B often affirm a radical equality and accentuate the dimension of order. The principle of freedom informed by excellence and the related notions of power and coercion are a source of major discomfort to proponents of this view. Hermits, religious seers and mystics of all types, as well as withdrawing sects such as the Amish and the Mennonites, illustrate this perspective.

Three Type II love-justice perspectives, which assume the interpenetration or contiguity of love and justice, are possible. Proponents of Type II-A argue that love should inform the world directly, but reject the idea that any general normative form of political or social organization or general principles of justice can be developed *a priori* from this affirmation of interpenetration. This rejection is coupled with a strong emphasis upon dynamics of "God's will," so the principles or patterns applicable in a particular context emerge from the interplay between the context and one's own past history.[3] The extremely strong emphasis on "God's will" (the dominance of dynamics or power) accounts for the elusiveness of principles of justice among protagonists of this perspective. Those who appeal to a theo-volitional principle almost always deny the participation of man's reason in ontic reason.

The other two Type II love-justice relations place a greater emphasis upon the aspect of form in human experience. If form is strongly dominant, a hierarchical pattern emerges; it dynamics is more significant, a more egalitarian pattern results. The former type is termed Type II-B; the latter, Type II-C. Roman Catholics have usually maintained Type II-B; Calvinist Protestants, Type II-C.[4]

Because the dominance of the dimension of form fosters a more rigid view of the hierarchical ordering of society, Roman Catholic social theorists have generally supported monarchy or aristocracy. Protestant social theorists, because an emphasis on dynamics leads to a more fluid view of the hierarchical ordering of society, have usually supported democracy. Some Presbyterian versions have upheld representative democracy with some aristocratic tendencies; some Baptist versions have encouraged a more egalitarian democracy.

Both of these Type II views interpret justice as the form which love takes in the world; therefore, theorists desire monarchy, aristocracy or democracy, the "good" forms of political organization. In spite of this preference, perversions have frequently occurred. Classical Roman Catholic preference for monarchy has occasionally led that church to support or sanction tyrants or oligarchs, while Protestant support of democracy has sometimes fostered oligarchs or anarchy.

Both Type II-B and Type II-C are informed by the principles of equality and freedom, but differ in their interpretations of the relation between them. Type II-B emphasizes form and, therefore, places equality in the context of forms discerned in nature or society. One's "due" depends upon one's position in a hierarchy, and the rules and regulations of justice are developed by examining "final" causes visible in nature and society. Proponents can be fairly precise about the rules and regulations which guide one's freedom of choice. Because the doctors of the church are in a peculiar position to understand these matters, protagonists frequently assign a strong directive role to the church and an elite group within the church.

This view discourages social change, emphasizes order, and encourages a more traditional orientation toward life. Any revisions will center upon a reconsideration of what constitutes "nature" and "society" and upon a review of final cause in relation to self-realization. In this review, a protagonist may accentuate man's freedom over nature, as for example, in some current Roman Catholic discussions of birth control.

The dominance of form in Roman Catholic social ethics is the basis for the close historical relation between Roman Catholic and Lutheran social ethics. The legitimacy of authority in both classical Roman Catholicism and classical Lutheranism reflects a strong traditional bias, in spite of the rational component formally embodied in them. Because they see a contiguity between love and justice, Roman Catholic social theorists, however, have taken a more constructive attitude toward some civil law then classical Lutheran theologians.

Because of their greater stress on dynamics, proponents of Type II-C love-justice relations are less clear about the rules and regulations of justice than are proponents of Type II-B relations. Type II-C formulations challenge the rendering of one's "due" through either the Lutheran "orders of creation" or the Roman Catholic hierarchical patterning of the social order.

The contrast is also reflected in differences between the Lutheran and Calvinist doctrines of vocation. In the Lutheran version, a man is called to work "in" a vocation; in the Calvinist version, a man is called to work "through" his vocation. The former version reflects a conserving view of the social order; the latter, a transforming view.

The greater emphasis upon freedom understood as self-determination informed by excellence in Type II-C leads to a broader concept of equality and the emergence of democratic forms of political organization, for the basic problem in the quest for justice becomes one of harmonizing or ordering the other two principles of justice. Form is dominant in the rational idea of equality appropriate to form, but dynamics is dominant in the notion of freedom understood as self-determination informed by excellence. The two principles are partly incompatible; although man is lured by love, he does not respond in perfect love, according to Protestant protagonists of Type II-C love-justice relations. Since freedom of choice in its formal sense does not correspond to freedom of choice in its material sense, one experiences an "isness-oughtness" contrast, due to finitude, ignorance and/or sin.

Man's inability to respond in perfect harmony of life with life leads some Protestant theorists of Type II-C to the judgment that some form of democracy is the best political structure man can devise to harmonize these partially conflicting but equally necessary principles of justice.[5] This understanding has contributed to the close historical affiliation of facets of Calvinism with democratic movements.

Any effort to build excellence into the social structure requires some institutionalization of aristocracy. Both Roman Catholicism and Calvinism have cultivated aristocratic groups. The College of Cardinals and the Board of Elders are attempts to institutionalize especially informed and sensitive ecclesiastical groups, just as the Senate of the United States represents an effort to institutionalize excellence in the political order.

The final major love-justice relation is one in which one of the notions is subsumed by the other. Two variants of the Type III option are possible. Proponents of Type III-A seek to realize the vision or experience of perfect harmony by reconstructing the world into the model which they envision. Proponents of Type III-B identify the character of the world in a particular epoch more or less unqualifiedly with the notion of perfection or with the relative "best" which mankind may attain.

Proponents of Type III-A generate movements which may be termed transforming sectarian movements. Various idealistic movements such as non-pragmatic pacifism, some socialist movements, facets of the contemporary civil rights movement in the United States, and the Münsterites of the Reformation illustrate this type. The protagonist holds tenaciously to a view of the perfection which he wants to see manifest in a reformed and reconstructed world. If love and justice are realized perfectly, then equality would correspond with one's due and formal and material freedom would coincide. Protagonists of this view may either ignore the problems related to this hypothetical harmonization or hold that a change in attitudes or in social structure or in both can induce perfect harmony of life with life. Protagonists of Type III-A love-justice relations are usually not systematic theologians or philosophers, but charismatic leaders whose followers value the style of their lives and their passionate convictions more than the coherence of their ideas.

Proponents of Type III-B generate socially conservative movements and are tradition-oriented. They minimize the idea of transcendent harmony and emphasize the *status quo* or an earlier "better" age. Because the pattern to which protagonists appeal cannot be delineated formally, no *a priori* statement of the relation which they envision between equality and freedom can be made.

In the United States, protagonists of this perspective have usually accentuated self-determination and order and have restricted the meaning of equality. The John Birch Society, minority segments of the National Association of Manufacturers and other conservative right-wing groups illustrate this type.

Both Type I relations, by rejecting the possibility of the world's transformation, minimize social change. In time, withdrawing groups (Type I-B) tend to become either radically revolutionary (Type III-A) or tradition-oriented (Type III-B). It is fairly easy to turn from a rejection of power and an attempt to build a more perfect community through a radical withdrawal from the world to an understanding which encourages the use of power to effect a radical transformation of the world. Or, one may institutionalize certain patterns over a period of time and adhere rigidly to them. Historically, many withdrawing groups reveal a strange blending of idealistic and traditionalistic characteristics.

This section has been focused upon the principles of justice. It is necessary to consider briefly the relation between the principles of justice and the more specific regulations of justice which provide direction in concrete situations.

Proponents of the various options just outlined will tend either toward contextualism and "spontaneity" in morality or toward carefully developed formal principles to guide man's moral behavior. Although they differ in shape and emphasis, proponents of Type I-A and Type II love-justice relations will consider both factors. If they emphasize form, they may develop specific rules and regulations to guide the quest for justice. If they emphasize dynamics, they will attain much less clarity. Some will note the interplay between the principles of justice and the life of a living community in the development of the rules and regulations of justice.

The rules and regulations of justice which emerge are once again unification of form, the principles of justice, and dynamics, the life of a living community. To trace this fusion in detail it would be necessary to move from the formal considerations guiding this discussion to a consideration of the concrete empirical dimensions of a particular society. The concrete manifestation of the "power" or dynamic component of the Trinity is directly involved in these dimensions, just as it is involved in the formal development of the principles of justice. The unification of form and dynamics at a concrete level also involves a lure toward the harmony related to the love component of the trinitarian structure of reality.

As these relations suggest, two other factors must be considered when moving from a formal discussion of love-justice relations to an analysis of the processes by which justice is realized in a concrete situation. The first factor is the dynamic aspect of the environment to which the rules and regulations of justice refer. Because the environment is constantly changing, justice is always evolving. This emergent form of justice may be more adequate, as adequate, or less adequate for the new context than the old form of justice.

The second factor is the formal aspect of the environment to which the rules and regulations of justice refer. A society guided by the notions of equality and self-determination informed by excellence may be expected to manifest more justice than does one informed by less adequate principles of justice.

Sociological analysis may provide guidance to those concerned with the realization of greater justice, for it may reveal inordinate inequality, discover factors limiting man's creative use of his potentialities as he manifests his self-determination, and suggest patterns to increase harmony.

Any analyst must use a guiding perspective related to options delineated in either this or the first chapter. Most contemporary sociologists do not employ the fundamental transcendental interpretations of reality which undergird the typology used in this chapter. Many contemporary sociologists agree with Thrasymachus, the Greek sophist who raised the question of justice in Book One of *The Republic*, that justice is the interest of the stronger. Max Weber, for example, is explicit upon this point in his interpretation of law and power. Others interpret justice with the aid of a reward-punishment mechanism. Talcott Parsons, for example, uses a gratification-deprivation model to interpret human motivation.[6]

In spite of these contrasts, the pervasiveness of "equality" and "freedom" as principles of justice in the United States fosters convergences at low levels of abstraction between protagonists whose fundamental views vary sharply. In the long run, it is doubtful if either an interest-of-the-stronger theory or a rewards-punishment schematism can sustain the human spirit. Other informing perspectives need to be nurtured. The concluding section outlines one such alternative.

A Constructive Interpretation of Love, Justice and Forms of Social Organization

THE LURE OF PERFECTION

Man has always been haunted by the lure of perfect harmony. The intuition of an ultimate harmony of harmonies is reflected in the folk literature of all literate peoples and in the oral traditions of non-literate peoples. Philosophers or theologians who reject this vision may be set in relation to such a perfection, for the negation of this intuition of perfection may be interpreted as a response to this pervasive vision.

Religious virtuosos, spirits who are particularly sensitive to intuitive insights, have sought to inform mankind of the magnitude of their vision by word and deed. Men have responded to their lure by developing rituals, institutions, and belief systems which have sought to encourage sensitive human response to this vision.

In addition to this intuition of perfection, the experience of mankind also points to an intrinsic interrelatedness of the cosmos: men are literally community-in-individuality. The dominant theological traditions of the West have been unwilling to apply this thorough-going principle of relativity to God, but if one grants the ultimate wisdom of the affirmation "God is love," there is nothing inherent in this tradition which would preclude applying the principle of relativity to God.

The sociability of human relations has usually been presupposed in the common experience of mankind. Negation requires great intellectual and emotive effort, as in the case of some mystics and seers. The tremendous difficulty which proponents of world-denying views encounter may lead one to suggest that their affirmation that the world is illusory is itself an illusion.

Two other fundamental facets of human experience must be set alongside the intuition of perfection and the fact of relationship. First, the intuition of an ultimate perfection is always a vision; it is never an actuality. The failure of some to fathom the relation of potentiality to actuality has led to the most heinous crimes in the name of one religion or another, to the emergence of fanatical sects of all types, and to the inability of pious men to effect reasonable compromise in personal, social, economic, cultural, political and religious life. Second, human experience inevitably incorporates the lure for harmony, the experience of forms or ideas, the actuality of the past, and the emergence of a new creation inextricably related to the reality of both the past and the future.

The emergence of a new creation encompasses form, dynamics, and unification from which the principles of justice are derived. The component of form in human experience gives rise to the idea of principles in general, fosters the notion of equality in particular as a principle of justice, and contributes to the differentiations which shape the rules and regulations of justice. The component of dynamics in human experience reflects the fundamental notion of creativity which is at the base of things, occasions the notion of self-determination as a principle of justice, and also contributes to the differentiations which shape the rules and regulations of justice. The lure for harmony and intensity of feeling reflected in human experience assures the becoming of *some* thing, leads to the notion of order as a principle of justice, and qualifies the rules and regulations of justice.

The intrinsic interrelatedness of form, dynamics and unification results in some modification of equality, self-determination, and order as principles of justice. Equality appropriate to form becomes one principle of justice; self-determination informed by excellence, a second; and order which harmonizes equality appropriate to form and self-determination informed by excellence, a third.

The transcendent lure for harmony introduces an "isness-oughtness" contrast. Men have centered their efforts to interpret this phenomenon around three loci—finitude, ignorance, and sin. Attention is now directed to this issue.

THE "ISNESS-OUGHTNESS" CONTRAST IN HUMAN EXPERIENCE

Finitude contributes to man's experience of disharmony and elicits an "isness-oughtness" contrast in three ways. First, it is the cause of loss, for life from the human point of view is inexorably transitory. Those moments of greatest joy and harmony in human experience unfortunately fade into the dim recesses of memory and past fact; those moments of greatest sorrow and disharmony fortunately also fade. In either case there is loss from the human point of view.[7]

Second, the very fact of realization means exclusion: other possibilities which might have been are excluded by the actualization of that which is. All realization, and thus all perfection, is finite. There is no such thing as one mode of perfection in the cosmos; rather, a variety of possibilities, each more or less appropriate for its context, will be actualized in due season.

Third, finitude contributes to the disharmony inherent in a particular context because past decisions condition the type and degree of harmony which can be attained in a given context. Lethargy and ignorance combine to dissuade one from efforts to do the good; the past experiences of the race or of the individual affect the social, economic, cultural, political and religious orders in a particular society; and the general natural environment which reflects a multiplicity of sub-human decisions may limit sharply the degree of harmony which can be attained in a particular context.

Ignorance obscures man's conceptual envisagement of the good and of the forms which would induce a higher harmony or perfection and, coupled with finitude, precludes his full knowledge of contingent phenomena which might induce the greatest possible harmony in a given situation. If philosophers were kings, the most appropriate harmony possible might be actualized, for each would contribute his appropriate share to the society and would receive his appropriate due from it. Philosophers, however, are not kings, and mankind agonizes.

Finally, some have employed sin or hybris to explain man's experience of imperfection. They appeal to man's primal and inordinate willful self-centeredness to explain the contrast between his experience of perfection and the disharmony apparent in his personal and corporate life. Although all the limitations on existence occasioned by finitude and ignorance delineated here are affirmed and the pervasiveness of inordinate self-centeredness among men is acknowledged, the doctrine of original sin and the related doctrine of creation *ex nihilo*, either in their classical form or in the modern forms developed or reaffirmed by contemporary Protestant theologians such as Karl Barth, Emil Brunner, and Reinhold Niebuhr, are rejected.

Once finitude and ignorance are acknowledged, it necessarily follows that disharmony is an inevitable part of human existence. It is not clear what the doctrine of sin contributes to illuminating the "isness-ought-ness" contrast. A higher and richer harmony of life with life may be attained with vision and effort. As the entertainment of such a possibility certainly does not assure its realization, this view most emphatically does not imply either inevitable human progress or the elimination of disharmony.

If love were or could be manifest unqualifiedly in the world, the issue of the love-justice relation would disappear. In a perfect world (if there be such), the problem would not emerge; in the world of human experience, it arises forcefully. That facet of love embodied in the experience of ultimate perfection initially creates the question of the relation between love and justice, for perfection is unattainable in the world.

Because of finitude and ignorance, the development of the principles of justice in human society is fraught with difficulty. Equality appropriate to form and self-determination informed by excellence cannot be perfectly reconciled; forms change, self-determination is lured by a multiplicity of possibilities, and men evade both thought and excellence.

The contrast between the lure for perfection and man's experience is accentuated even more when one moves from the general principles of justice to specific rules and regulations of justice. The rules of justice are only more or less adequate to a given situation; and, for good or ill, human beings customarily try to evade some of the rules which are established in a living community. The final portion of this volume is devoted to an attempted reconciliation of these principles of justice and suggestions as to the contribution which religious institutions and religious professionals may make to the quest for justice.

EQUALITY, SELF-DETERMINATION AND ORDER: AN INTERPRETATION

Finitude and ignorance create an inevitable contrast between the vision of perfection and justice, so it is essential to discover principles of justice to guide mankind in the quest for greater harmony in the body politic. There are three such principles. A formal or rational principle of equality appropriate to form is derived from the conceptual side of human experience. A dynamic principle of freedom in the sense of self-determination informed by the lure for excellence is derived from the process side of human experience. A harmonizing principle of order is derived from the pervasive experience of a lure of harmony and a vision of perfection.

Equality appropriate to form as a principle of justice is qualified by the emergence of new forms, the hierarchical ordering of organisms, and the ascribed and achieved differentiations among human beings. It is not unequivocally clear, therefore, among whom the principle of equality should apply even though common human creaturehood and one's inextricable relations with others accentuate this principle.

The principle of self-determination informed by excellence further obscures the situation, for this principle is only partially reconcilable with the principle of equality appropriate to form. The dynamic character of this principle is limited by the principle of equality.

The principle of order involves harmonizing the other two principles of justice. It also introduces the notion "appropriate to form" to the principle of equality and the notion "informed by excellence" to the principle of self-determination. Some general guidelines for reconciling freedom and equality can be delineated, but the details can be resolved only in the interaction between the principles of justice and the life of a living community.

The principle of equality requires that the law should apply equally to all who fall under its domain. Although it certainly should mitigate gross inequality, the principle of equality cannot be extended unqualifiedly to include unequivocal equality of income, housing, cultural and educational opportunity, political power, and so on, for self-determination informed by excellence partially contradicts the principle of equality.

The vision of the more excellent way of love and the appropriation of the proper forms by all creatures would assure that self-determination informed by excellence and equality appropriate to form would harmonize supremely in an ideal world with a single type of perfection. In the actual world of finitude, ignorance, and a multiplicity of perfections, the two principles do not coalesce; therefore, the dynamic principle of self-determination must be contrasted with the formal rational principle of equality.

Some inequality in a society is inevitable. The way in which these partially disharmonious principles of equality and self-determination are balanced cannot be determined formally, but the balance will emerge in the give-and-take of a living community. A consensus between conflicting persons and groups may frequently be reached voluntarily. Sometimes issues cannot be resolved voluntarily and have to be resolved by the coercive power of the state, the organizing center of a society.

When considering the rational principle of equality in connection with the pervasiveness of community-in-individuality, a multiplicity of perfections, finitude, and ignorance, one is led to the judgment that limitations should be placed upon inequality of wealth, power and opportunity in a society but that such inequalities cannot and should not be eliminated. The notion of finite perfections or excellence, each more or less appropriate to its context, precludes too narrow an interpretation of equality or too mediocre an understanding of self-determination.

The vision of excellence needs to be vigorously emphasized in connection with self-determination, for it can transform the principle of self-determination into a higher and more meaningful one. The fact of community-in-individuality, coupled with this lure toward higher excellence and the principles of justice, provides some guidance for appropriate self-determination in a given context. These are the factors which have contributed to the meaning of freedom in its many senses which is characteristic of higher civilizations.

Self-determination informed by excellence and equality appropriate to form are unified more or less adequately in a given society. This unification is effected by the principle of order. As with the other two principles of justice, order cannot be made absolute. Too much order may jeopardize emergent novelty and maintain relative injustice, but too little order may undercut the stability of a congenial sustaining environment upon which the cultural achievements of higher civilizations depend.

Equality, self-determination, and order are not perfectly realizable at any time or in any place. Despite the absence of perfect compatability, one may delineate the forms of social organization which most adequately harmonize equality and self-determination. Even though such a vision is not relevant in all human societies and cannot be perfectly realized in any human society, it can serve to sustain mankind in its quest for justice. This delineation is based on both categorical notions and contingent phenomena. The categorical notions are the principles of justice; the contingent phenomena, the characteristics of mankind.

The family is grounded in man's need for intimacy, in his personal unity, and in the bisexuality of the species. For creatures with these natural characteristics, monogamy is the form of family organization which can most adequately balance equality and self-determination.

The economic sphere is founded on man's physical needs and his rational and creative capacities. Because it accentuates the rational component, the economic sphere does not involve man's total being as does the family. This limited involvement does not exclude the economic sphere from moral evaluation, but it does prevent any categorical judgment about the best possible form of economic organization. A desirable form of economic organization must foster responsible economic growth and must have a pricing mechanism so that supply and demand are regulated with reasonable efficiency. However, a number of forms of economic organization may meet this requirement. This system must also permit men to exercise a measure of self-determination and risk-taking. Again, however, several forms of economic organization may meet this requirement. The form of economic organization most compatible with the principles of justice can be better described by negative than by positive characteristics. Economic systems which foster excessive laissez-faire practices or excessive central planning are suspect *a priori*, but what is excessive cannot be discerned independent of a given context.

The triad of principles of justice suggests the desirability of a limited cultural pluralism in a society. Both equality appropriate to form and self-determination informed by excellence foster cultural pluralism, but the principle of order limits such pluralism. Too little pluralism is stifling; too much, disruptive.

Representative democracy is the form of political organization which can most adequately harmonize equality appropriate to form and self-determination informed by excellence. A federal system of representative democracy is the best form of political organization mankind has yet been able to envision or realize to cope with the ambiguity inherent in the dual principles of justice, both of which are related to the principle of harmony. Although some disharmony between the two principles is unavoidable, democracy encourages, but does not guarantee, the flowering of self-determination informed by excellence and permits, but does not demand, the extension of equality appropriate to form.[8]

The religious sphere arises from man's response to his synthesis of physical and conceptual feelings, from his intuition of the order and harmony at the conceptual base of things, and from his response to the Supreme Entity Who lures him to become and Who receives his being perfectly and everlastingly. Because of finitude, ignorance and the ultimate dominance of a supra-rational dimension in the nature of things, absolute certainty about religious belief systems is impossible. Nevertheless, some measure of certainty is attainable. Since man is rooted in history, religious meaning and feeling is mediated to him by a particular or a limited number of traditions. Therefore, a limited pluralism of religious institutions is desirable. Because of this legitimate pluralism and man's capacity for self-determination, the state should not coerce religious expression. Religious liberty is one of the hallmarks of a civilized society, and freedom of choice among several religious institutions is a prized value.

Although critics may allege that these formulations are excessively conditioned by structures extant in American society, it is maintained here that the forms are generally desirable. Considerable room for variety within and among the several spheres exists. It is not possible to develop any *a priori* judgments about these variations, for the context and the life history of peoples condition the shape of an appropriate form.

These social forms have been more adequately institutionalized in western, liberal democracies than in other human societies. Even though these forms are not relevant to all contemporary human societies, they may serve as a lure to mankind in his perennial quest for love and justice.

Because the political sphere deals directly with the problem of community-in-individuality, it is especially crucial in shaping the life of a human society. Because its responsibilities are transrational (not irrational), it properly occupies a position superior to the economic sphere. The government may legitimately intervene in the economic sphere, but the intervention should be guided both by theoretical considerations about the efficiency of a given economic system and by political judgments about the desirability of alternative allocations of economic resources.

In the United States, universal suffrage, a legislative body apportioned according to population, universal free education, and a legal system based on the principle of equality before the law foster the principle of equality appropriate to form. Federalism, a legislative body apportioned according to geography, the basic structure of democracy as self-government, cultural pluralism, religious liberty, wealth differentials sustained by a modified enterprise economic system, and ability differentials related to man's biological substructure and to facets of all the spheres of the social order foster the principle of self-determination informed by excellence. The balance between the two principles emerges from their interaction in a community.

The secular trend in the United States is characterized by the progressive but uneven extension of some facets of equality and the progressive limitations of some facets of self-determination. Although self-determination informed by excellence frequently may demand the extension of equality and self-limitation, it is likely that the principle of self-determination will be seriously threatened in the long run. The danger to self-determination arises from a pervasive technical rationalism. This rationalism is especially evident in the economic sphere, but is also strongly emphasized in the other spheres. It is accentuated by the fragmentation of social relations fostered by urbanization, bureaucratization and industrialization and by the atomization of experience fostered by mass media.[9] Although urbanization, industrialization, bureaucratization and the extension of equality are interpreted here in an ambiguously positive manner, there are many difficulties in such trends because man's humanity is related to but transcends technical rationalism and equality.

Ambiguity is present, for example, in the emergence of the prodigiously productive economic system now characteristic of the United States. It has freed many men of tedious tasks and has subsequently enhanced some forms of self-determination; concomitantly, it has led men into an intricately interrelated mechanical and electronic dependence and has reduced other forms of self-determination.

Fashionable contemporary analyses of American religious institutions which criticize their adjustive and integrative functions, such as Peter Berger's *The Noise of Solemn Assemblies* and Gibson Winter's *The Suburban Captivity of the Churches,* lack balance because the forms of social organization which have been institutionalized in the United States warrant the qualified support of religious professionals.[10] Despite much complacency and lethargy among Americans, the pervasive conditioning effects of the economic sphere on the style of life and value orientations of the American people and the painfully evident perversions and mediocrities in all spheres, it is appropriate for religious institutions to support, with qualifications, the fundamental structures of American society.

Those in the Calvinist tradition must reject sharply negative interpretations of religious life in the United States, for many of the values which facets of the Calvinist tradition hoped to institutionalize have been incorporated in the values and social structures of the United States. Although religious professionals may make responsible criticisms and innovating suggestions within an affirmation of American values and social structures, religious institutions in the United States should function in a dominantly adjustive and integrative manner.

Many Christians *qua* citizens entertain alternative views on many major political and economic issues in the United States, but some persons suggest that the Church should be in the world confronting "power structures."[11] This position must be challenged, for most economic and political action in a democracy is ambiguous. A perennial contrast between equality appropriate to form and self-determination informed by excellence, both of which bear an ambiguous relation to love, makes it extremely difficult to state a Christian position on many specific issues. The difficulty is accentuated by the ambiguous relation of the principles to the rules of justice incorporated in the legal order and to the application of these rules in a particular situation. Because of this ambiguity at every level, the greatest reserve is necessary when identifying a particular stance or cause as peculiarly "Christian" in a society in which democracy is institutionalized and functioning tolerably well. In such a society, critical and innovating centers are dispersed throughout the society and are not a peculiar property of the Church.

The Church does not have a special claim on God's activity in the Universe and does not represent a categorically unique locus for God's relation to the world. Nevertheless, its focus on the transcendent and primordial facet of God's nature and on worship does provide some guidance for its relations with the other spheres of the social order. The Church is not merely one voluntary association among others; rather, it is an institution whose reason for existence is to foster worship, education and socialization among its members and to lure them to service and the quest for justice.

In spite of the word of caution just advanced, the principles of justice do provide some guidance for judgments on social, economic and political issues. Extreme positions must be subjected to the closest scrutiny; policies, laws or programs which inordinately emphasize either the principle of equality or of self-determination are *a priori* suspect.

Although a consideration of the principles of justice allows for sharp criticism of extreme positions, the principles do not provide such a clear evaluation of more moderate positions. Various rules of justice may serve the cause of justice, and legitimate differences may exist among those who affirm common principles of justice.

The extension of the political franchise to all who can exercise a degree of responsible self-determination, for example, receives high priority in the United States for all the principles of justice coverge on this point. Those areas of the United States which deny such elemental political equality and which do not provide the facilities to sustain the development of citizens who can exercise responsible self-determination are rightly subject to the sharpest criticism, but the development of rules and structures of justice which will insure extension of the franchise is difficult. A variety of approaches is possible; differences which develop among various groups may be adjudicated by political compromise or, ultimately, by the coercive power of the federal government.

As observed earlier, the political sphere is crucial in human affairs because it deals directly with the problem of community-in-individuality. Both intra-state and inter-state relations are of utmost importance for the quest for justice and the survival of mankind.

Although a clear-cut distinction between democratic and non-democratic countries is obviously spurious, a great contrast does exist between those nations where democracy is functioning tolerably well and those countries where despotism is most evident. As differences in the religious belief systems and in fundamental value orientations are intertwined with these differences of political organization, significant changes in the political organization in many areas of the world are unlikely in the foreseeable future. Democrats must balance their persuasion that democracy is the best possible form of political organization with an awareness of its lack of relevance in many areas of the world for a long time to come.

Even the existence of a world composed only of sovereign democracies would provide no reasonable assurance of international tranquility. If mankind is to survive, some form of international coordinating agency only barely foreseeable at the present time must emerge in the coming decades. Mankind will be unable to attain a modicum of love and justice without patience, roughly comparable military deterrence by the major powers, willingness to experiment with novel forms, and concern for human welfare.

Religious professionals in the United States may contribute most significantly to man's quest for justice by presenting a vision of desirable forms of social organization, witnessing to the eternal lure of Divine harmony, trying to develop more adequate manifestations of democracy, and sustaining appropriate individual self-expression of excellence in all the spheres of man's life together.

Notes

Notes to Introduction

1. Though the quest for universal propositions true for any possible subject is important and necessary, limitations of insight and the inadequate and elliptical nature of language prevent the complete attainment of this objective. Systematic consideration of such universal propositions, properly termed metaphysical, is beyond the scope of this book.

2. For a fuller discussion of this and related issues, see W. Widick Schroeder, "The Ordering of the Sciences in the Perspective of Process Philosophy," in W. Alvin Pitcher, editor, *Social Ethics: Problems and Promises* (Chicago: University of Chicago Press, in preparation).

Notes to Chapter I

1. This chapter is based upon an article entitled "Cognitive Structures and Religious Research," which appeared in the *Review of Religious Research*, III, No. 2 (Fall, 1961), 72-81.

2. Floyd Hunter, *Community Power Structure* (Chapel Hill: University of North Carolina Press, 1954).

3. Ernst Barker, *Reflections on Government* (New York: Oxford University Press, 1958).

4. See, for example, the theoretic distinctions made by Paul H. Furfey in *The Scope and Method of Sociology* (New York: Harper & Bros., 1953) or Joseph H. Fichter in *Sociology* (Chicago: University of Chicago Press, 1957). Fichter's descriptive empirical studies may be interpreted in this context. His concern with human freedom of choice and his resistance to Freudian interpretations of human motivation may have contributed to the ordering of his empirical material.

5. See, for example, George Herbert Mead, *Mind, Self, and Society* (Chicago: University of Chicago Press, 1934) and Walter Coutu, *Emergent Human Nature* (New York: A. A. Knopf, 1949). Sidney Hook, *The Hero in History* (New York: The John Day Co., 1943) is an interesting philosophic formulation in a similar perspective.

6. See Sigmund Freud, *Moses and Monotheism* (London: The Hogarth Press and the Institute of Psycho-Analysis, 1939), *New Introductory Lectures on Psycho-Analysis* (New York: W. W. Norton & Co., Inc., 1933), *The Future of an Illusion* (Great Britain: Horace Liveright and The Institute of Psycho-Analysis, 1928), *Civilization and Its Discontents* (London: The Hogarth Press, 1951); and Emile Durkheim, *Sociology and Philosophy* (Glencoe, Illinois: The Free Press, 1953) and *The Elementary Forms of the Religious Life* (London: G. Allen & Unwin, Ltd.; New York: Macmillan, 1915).

7. See, for example, the treatment of religion in W. Lloyd Warner, *Democracy in Jonesville* (New York: Harper & Bros., 1949) and *The Family of God* (New Haven: Yale University Press, 1961); Kingsley Davis, *Human Society* (New York: Macmillan Co., 1949); J. Milton Yinger, *Religion, Society, and the Individual* (New York: Macmillan, 1957) and *Sociology Looks at Religion* (New York: Macmillan, 1963); Robin Williams, *American Society* (New York: A. A. Knopf, 1951); Weston LaBarre, *The Human Animal* (Chicago: University of Chicago Press, 1954); Thomas Hoult, *Sociology of Religion* (New York: Dryden Press, 1958); Talcott Parsons, *The Social System* (Glencoe, Illinois: The Free Press, 1951), and most other contemporary works in the field.

8. The recent reorganization and renaming of the *American Catholic Sociological Review* poses some interesting problems. As noted earlier, the distinctions between the theoretic and the practical disciplines might well encourage sociologists who affirm the Thomistic perspective to achieve a limited consensus with sociologists in other traditions. However, continued disagreement in certain areas must be expected. It is interesting to speculate on the sociological significance of the increased rapprochement between Catholic sociologists and the bulk of the profession. It is likely that many Catholic sociologists are in the process of appropriating new cognitive structures.

9. See Reinhold Niebuhr, *The Nature and Destiny of Man* (New York: Charles Scribner's Sons, 1949); Paul Tillich, *Systematic Theology* (Chicago: University of Chicago Press, 1951, 1955, 1963); and Alfred N. Whitehead, *Process and Reality* (New York: Macmillan, 1929).

Notes to Chapter II

1. See, for example, the interesting convergence of interpretations of international relations between Reinhold Niebuhr, *The Structure of Nations and Empires* (New York: Charles Scribner's Sons, 1960) and Hans Morgenthau, *Politics Among Nations* (New York: A. Knopf, 1948). Niebuhr sets his interpretation in contrast to an ultimate harmony while Morgenthau limits his interpretation to the study of political phenomena.

2. See especially W. Lloyd Warner and Paul S. Lunt, *The Social Life of a Modern Community* (New Haven: Yale University Press, 1941), and W. Lloyd Warner and associates, *Democracy in Jonesville.* Other relevant studies include N. J. Demerath III, *Social Class in American Protestantism* (Chicago: Rand McNally, 1965); A. B. Hollingshead, *Elmtown's Youth* (New York: J. Wiley, 1949); Gerhard Lenski, *The Religious Factor* (Garden City: Doubleday & Com-

pany, 1961); Liston Pope, "Religion and the Class Structure," *The Annals*, No. 256, (March, 1948) 84-91; and W. Widick Schroeder and Victor Obenhaus, *Religion in American Culture* (New York: The Free Press, 1964).

3. For an evocative discussion of this problem, See Gerhard Lenski, "American Social Classes: Statistical Strata or Social Groups?" *American Journal of Sociology*, LVIII (September, 1952), 139-144.

4. See, for example, Gerhard Lenski, *The Religious Factor* and W. Widick Schroeder and Victor Obenhaus, *Religion in American Culture*.

5. See, for example, C. Wright Mills, *White Collar* (New York: Oxford University Press, 1951); C. Wright Mills, *The Power Elite* (New York: Oxford University Press, 1956); W. Lloyd Warner and associates, *Democracy in Jonesville;* and W. Lloyd Warner, *The Family of God*.

6. For an extended discussion of these relations see Chapters XI and XII.

7. See Chapter XII for a fuller explication of these issues and for a definition of the principles of justice cited in the following paragraph.

Notes to Chapter III

1. This chapter is based upon an article entitled "Conceptualizations of Urbanization and Urbanism" which appeared in the *Review of Religious Research*, V, NO. 2, (Winter, 1964), 74-79.

2. See Chapter VII for a fuller discussion of this issue.

3. Max Weber, *The City* translated and edited by Don Martindale and Gertrude Neuwirth (Glencoe, Illinois: The Free Press, 1958).

4. *Ibid.*, p. 62.

5. See, for example, Reinhold Niebuhr, *The Nature and Destiny of Man*. The "isness-oughtness" contrast in the Christian tradition is also found in the Platonic tradition. Platonists regard finitude and ignorance as the sources of disharmony in the world.

6. Maurice R. Stein, *The Eclipse of Community: An Interpretation of American Studies* (Princeton: Princeton University Press, 1960). In the latter part of this work, this issue is complicated by Stein's use of the Freudian perspective.

7. *Ibid.*, pp. 99-101. Lewis Mumford's great works on the city are also set in this interactionalist-operationalist tradition. This chapter limits references to exemplary cases.

8. Louis Wirth, "Urbanism as a Way of Life,' *American Journal of Sociology*, XLIV, No. 1 (July, 1938), 1-24.

9. *Ibid.*, pp. 7-8.

10. *Ibid.*, p. 8.

11. *Ibid.*, pp. 8-9. The italics have been added.

12. An extended discussion of these issues is found in Chapter VIII which deals with Talcott Parsons. Both Wirth and Parsons employ an analysis of components.

13. Protestant theologians informed by neo-Kantian views frequently develop a tripartite ordering of the sciences. Although the division is based on the

nature of man rather than on the nature of the subject matter, a comparable normative form of social organization emerges. Emil Brunner, for example, holds up the principle of federalism as the guide in social organization. (See, for example, Emil Brunner, *Justice and the Social Order*, translated by Mary Bottinger [New York and London: Harper and Brothers, 1945].)

Notes to Chapter IV

1. This chapter is based upon an article entitled "Lay Expectations of the Ministerial Role: An Exploration of Protestant-Catholic Differentials," which appeared in the *Journal for the Scientific Study of Religion*, II, No. 2 (Spring, 1963), 217-227.

2. In this chapter, the full-time religious professional is one who by ecclesiastical order, by consensus of the religious institution, or both is responsible for a religious institution. The empirical focus is upon Protestant ministers and Roman Catholic priests related to local congregations in two communities in a Corn Belt county in the United States.

3. The following works were especially helpful in formulating the framework employed in this analysis and in developing the Protestant-Catholic comparisons of the ministry:

Thomas Aquinas, *Selected Writings* (New York: E. P. Dutton & Co., 1939).

Aurelius Augustine, *The Confessions of St. Augustine* (New York: Sheed and Ward, 1943).

Chester I. Barnard, *The Functions of the Executive* (Cambridge: Harvard University Press, 1938).

Karl Barth, *The Word of God and the Word of Man* (Boston, Chicago: The Pilgrim Press, 1928), especially Chapter 4.

Emil Brunner, *The Divine Imperative* (London: The Lutterworth Press, 1937).

John Calvin, *Institutes of the Christian Religion* (Philadelphia: Westminster Press, 1960), especially Book IV.

Joseph H. Fichter, *Religion as an Occupation: A Study in the Sociology of Professions* (Notre Dame: University of Notre Dame Press, 1961).

Everett C. Hughes, *Men and Their Work* (Glencoe: The Free Press, 1958).

H. Richard Niebuhr and Daniel D. Williams, eds., *The Ministry in Historical Perspectives* (New York: Harper & Bros., 1956).

H. Richard Niebuhr in collaboration with Daniel D. Williams and James M. Gustafson, *The Purpose of the Church and Its Ministry* (New York: Harper & Bros., 1956).

Talcott Parsons, *The Social System.*

Max Weber, *From Max Weber: Essays in Sociology* (New York: Oxford University Press, 1946).

Alfred N. Whitehead, *Adventures of Ideas* (New York: Macmillan, 1933), especially Chapter 4.

Alfred N. Whitehead, *Process and Reality.*

4. See Chapter XI for one interpretation of a religious professional's role in contemporary American society.

5. Additional findings from this study have been reported in other publications. See Victor Obenhaus, W. Widick Schroeder and Charles D. England, "Church Participation Related to Social Class and Type of Center," *Rural Sociology,* XXIII (September, 1958), 298-308; Victor Obenhaus and W. Widick Schroeder "Church Affiliation and Attitudes Toward Selected Public Questions in a Typical Midwest County," *Rural Sociology,* XXVIII (March, 1963), 35-47; Victor Obenhaus, *The Church and Faith in Mid-America* (Philadelphia: Westminster Press, 1963); and W. Widick Schroeder and Victor Obenhaus, *Religion in American Culture.*

6. For an objection to some of the dimensions which are incorporated in a professional religious leadership role and to some hypothesized lay expectations from the point of view of an apologist, see Joseph Sittler, *The Ecology of Faith* (Philadelphia: Muhlenberg Press, 1961).

7. These findings are compatible, at one level, with the interpretation of religion in American society advanced by Will Herberg and Gerhard Lenski. Both universalizing and individualizing factors are involved in the interplay between American society and the two major religious traditions. See Will Herberg, *Protestant, Catholic, Jew* (New York: Doubleday & Co., 1956), and Gerhard Lenski, *The Religious Factor.*

8. See W. Lloyd Warner, Marchia Meeker and Kenneth Eells, *Social Class in America: A Manual of Procedure for the Measurement of Social Status* (Chicago: Science Research Associates, 1949).

9. It is necessary to say certain things to establish some elements for contrast, but because this chapter is focused upon empirical findings, it is not possible to deal systematically with the issues here. See Parts Three and Four for a fuller explication of these issues.

10. Love-justice relations, which shape alternative Christian views of this matter, are considered in detail in Chapter XII.

11. It is beyond the scope of this chapter to deal with the different meanings of love in the Christian tradition and contemporary sociology. Love as *libido* is dominant in contemporary sociology, while other qualities are invariably introduced by Christian theologians. For a contemporary example, compare the understandings of love developed by Paul Tillich in *Love, Power and Justice* (New York: Oxford University Press, 1954) and by Talcott Parsons in *The Social System.* See Chapter VIII for a critical treatment of Parsons and Part Four for a more adequate consideration of the love-justice and God-world relations implicit in the discussion in this chapter.

Notes to Chapter V

1. For an extended and generally sympathetic treatment of The Woodlawn Organization, see Charles E. Silberman, *Crisis in Black and White* (New York: Random House, 1964).

2. The principle of "self-determination" as construed by The Woodlawn Organization stands in this tradition, as does Saul Alinsky's book, *Reveille For Radicals* (Chicago: University of Chicago Press, 1946). This fact is of interest because of the early relationship between Alinsky's Industrial Areas Foundation and The Woodlawn Organization.

3. Whether this situation can be modified significantly in the future is under debate. Many changes have taken place in the Catholic church in the past decade. For an evocative and polemical interpretation of the changing Catholic Church in the United States, see Edward Wakin and Father Joseph F. Scheuer, *The De-Romanization of the American Catholic Church* (New York: Macmillan, 1966).

The development of democracy has been associated historically with nations in the Calvinist tradition, though a complex of conditioning factors has contributed to the emergence of democracy in modern times. It is beyond the scope of this chapter to deal with this whole area.

4. See Chapters XI and XII for a systematic discussion of this issue.

5. These descriptive observations were accurate in 1967.

6. See Chapter XII for a systematic discussion of this issue.

Notes to Chapter VI

1. Emile Durkheim, *The Elementary Forms of the Religious Life; Sociology and Philosophy;* and *The Rules of Sociological Method* (Glencoe: The Free Press, 1938).

2. Emile Durkheim, *Sociology and Philosophy,* p. 4.

3. *Ibid.,* p. 4.

4. Emile Durkheim, *The Elementary Forms of the Religious Life.*

5. *Ibid.,* pp. 423-424.

6. The same universalization of fundamental components underlies Parsons' effort to develop an elaborate morphological structure. Parsons is considered in Chapter VIII.

7. Parsons confronts the same problem. See 109.

8. In the chapter, "The Determination of Moral Facts," *Sociology and Philosophy,* pp. 40-41, Durkheim makes the following observation:

Just as I am not concerned with the manner in which this or that particular individual sees morality, I also leave on one side the opinions of philosophers and moralists. I have nothing whatever to do with their systematic attempts to explain or construct moral reality except in so far as one can find in them a more or less adequate expression of the morality of their time. A moralist has a far greater sensibility than the average man to the dominant moral trends of his time, and consequently his consciousness is more representative of the moral reality. But I refuse to accept his doctrines as explanations, as scientific expressions of past or present moral reality.

9. Emile Durkheim, *Sociology and Philosophy,* pp. 88-89. Some theistic thinkers in the modern period have suggested that God does change in some ways.

10. Emile Durkheim, *The Elementary Forms of the Religious Life,* p. 444.

11. *Ibid.*, pp. 444-445.

12. A critical assessment of Durkheim's characterization of the development of philosophy and theology must be based upon some alternative perspective. From the point of view held here, Durkheim's views are suspect. The Platonic dialogues are more subtle and comprehensive than the philosophic formulations of most of Plato's successors, including Durkheim. An evolution of philosophic thought is equivocal, but the greater coordination of philosophic thought which has occurred does constitute a type of progress.

13. Emile Durkheim, *The Elementary Forms of the Religious Life*, p. 47.

14. *Ibid.*, p. 423.

15. *Ibid.*, p. 429.

16. *Ibid.*, pp. 430-431.

17. *Ibid.*, p. 446.

18. A comparison of Durkheim's formulations with those of Aristotle is useful. Aristotle sets the whole area of man and society in the practical realm, which he differentiates from both theoretic and aesthetic realms. Durkheim emphasizes society and minimizes the significance of the actions and decisions of men. Aristotle maintains a more careful balance between the two.

19. Emile Durkheim, *The Elementary Forms of the Religious Life*, p. 429.

20. This procedure is similar to Pareto's and is developed and refined by Parsons. See Chapter VIII for a further consideration and critique of this approach. This approach is most clear in *The Division of Labor in Society* (New York: Macmillan, 1933); *Suicide* (Glencoe: The Free Press, 1951); and in parts of *The Elementary Forms of the Religious Life.*

21. "Succeeded" is placed in quotes because this process of unification of physical and mental poles is out of time. Time itself is measured by the sequence of actual entities which become.

22. Emile Durkheim, *The Rules of Sociological Method*, p. 112.

Notes to Chapter VII

1. See H. H. Gerth and C. Wright Mills, translators and editors, *From Max Weber: Essays in Sociology*, pp. 77-156. All references are to this translation.

2. Max Weber, *The Theory of Social and Economic Organization*, translated by A. R. Henderson and Talcott Parsons (New York: Oxford University Press, 1947). All references are to this translation.

3. H. H. Gerth and C. Wright Mills, *From Max Weber: Essays in Sociology*, p. 144.

4. Max Weber, *The Theory of Social and Economic Organization*, pp. 108-109.

5. *Ibid.*, p. 88.

6. *Ibid.*, p. 152.

7. *Ibid.*, p. 156.

8. *Ibid.*, p. 158.

9. *Ibid.*, pp. 158-159.

10. *Ibid.*, pp. 109-111.

11. H. H. Gerth and C. Wright Mills, *From Max Weber: Essays in Sociology*, p. 143.

12. *Ibid.*, p. 141.

13. *Ibid.*, pp. 145-146.

14. *Ibid.*, p. 146.

15. *Ibid.*, p. 152.

16. *Ibid.*, p. 155.

17. *Ibid.*, p. 155.

18. *Ibid.*, p. 127.

19. *Ibid.*, pp. 153-154.

20. *Ibid.*, p. 147.

21. See, for example, the ordering of the sciences developed by Emile Brunner in Chapter II, "The Imminent Moral Phases of the Self," *The Divine Imperative*, and the structuring of the life of the church developed by James Gustafson in *Treasure in Earthen Vessels* (New York: Harper & Co., 1961). H. Richard Niebuhr's distinction between external and internal history in *The Meaning of Revelation* (New York: Macmillan, 1941) coheres with Weber's distinction between theoretic and practical reason.

22. See the final section of Chapter XII for the development of this viewpoint.

Notes to Chapter VIII

1. This chapter is based upon an article entitled "Talcott Parsons' Ordering of the Sciences: A Resume and a Critique" which appeared in the *Journal for the Scientific Study of Religion*, IV, No. 2 (Spring, 1965), 162-174.

2. Talcott Parsons, *The Social System.*

3. Talcott Parsons, *The Structure of Social Action* (New York: McGraw-Hill, 1937).

4. Talcott Parsons, *The Social System*, p. 328.

5. *Ibid.*, p. 335.

6. Talcott Parsons, *The Structure of Social Action*, p. 595.

7. *Ibid.*, pp. 597-599. The richness and complexity of human life, coupled with the complexity and novelty of human responses, introduce substantive differentiations which limit the usefulness of the analytical sciences which Parsons is attempting to develop here. The fundamental critique is developed in the last section of this chapter.

8. Talcott Parsons, *The Social System*, p. 547.

9. *Ibid.*, p. 550. It may be noted that this claim to autonomy of economic theory would be rejected by a variety of alternative theorists. They might also deny the fact-value distinctions and the logical-substantive distinctions which Parsons affirms, for the two issues are interrelated.

10. *Ibid.*, p. 555.

11. *Ibid.*, p. 552.

12. *Ibid.*, p. 553.

13. *Ibid.*, p. 20.

14. *Ibid.*, p. 328.

15. *Ibid.*, p. 329.
16. *Ibid.*, pp. 5-6.

Notes to Chapter IX

1. See the appropriate sections of Chapters VI, VII and VIII for a detailed consideration of the issues summarized here. The last section of each chapter is a critique of the sociologist under examination.

2. It is not coincidental that the work of C. Wright Mills took the direction it did. Mills' passionate concerns with sociology and politics are clearly in the tradition of Weber, to whom Mills is perhaps most indebted. See, for example, C. Wright Mills, *The Power Elite* and *The Sociological Imagination* (New York: Oxford University Press, 1959). Contemporary debates in sociology about structural-functional theory involve theoretical differences which are comparable to the differences between Weber and the other two philosophical sociologists discussed here.

Notes to Chapter X

1. For a contemporary expression of this general point of view, see Paul F. Lazarsfeld's foreword to Herbert Hyman's *Survey Design and Analysis* (Glencoe: The Free Press, 1960).

2. See Chapters XI and XII for a fuller discussion of these issues.

3. Alfred North Whitehead, *Process and Reality*, p. 67. Although his view of the nature of God-world relates differs from Whitehead's, Paul Tillich also reflects this rationalist viewpoint in the ontological analyses he undertakes in *Love, Power, and Justice.*

4. Because of Whitehead's understanding of the relation between reason, words and reality and of the ultimacy of the category of creativity, Whitehead's view is more Protestant than Catholic, for Thomistic rationalism emphasizes the primacy of being.

5. Reinhold Niebuhr, *The Nature and Destiny of Man*, I, p. 15. In Chapter V of the same volume, Niebuhr develops the distinction between man's understanding of God as Creator and Judge and man's understanding of God as Redeemer. He develops these ideas at great length in the first four chapters of the second volume.

6. Emil Brunner, *The Divine Imperative*, p. 10. Protagonists within this broad type may disagree on the role of phenomenological reason in theological work. For example, Karl Barth is critical of Brunner's attempt to develop a non-biblically centered phenomenological explication of the human situation to which he relates the Christian faith. Those guided by this third option are most likely to be critical of the typological efforts in this work because of their strong emphasis upon the dynamic aspects of reality and the relativity of human knowledge. See Chapter XI for a more inclusive consideration of the issues discussed in this section.

7. Gerhard Lenski, *The Religious Factor;* and Charles Y. Glock and Rod-

ney Stark, *Christian Beliefs and Anti-Semitism* (New York: Harper & Row, 1966).

Notes to Chapter XI

1. The author wants to acknowledge his debt to Charles Hartshorne and William L. Reese for their formulation of God-world relations. Because of the generality of the ideas of identity, overlap, contiguity, and independence on which this typology is based, it can readily be incorporated into theirs. Only formal considerations are developed here, so this typology does not deal with all of the dimensions which Hartshorne and Reese consider. See especially Charles Hartshorne, *Man's Vision of God* (New York: Harper, 1941); Charles Hartshorne and William L. Reese, *Philosophers Speak of God* (Chicago: University of Chicago Press, 1953); and Charles Hartshorne, *The Logic of Perfection* (La Salle, Illinois: The Open Court Press, 1963).

2. See especially Chapters I, II, and V. The full typology of alternative ontic perspectives is developed in this chapter. The references cited here are illustrative rather than exhaustive. For a perspectival approach to the social sciences which possesses analogs to the one used here, see Gibson Winter, *Elements for a Social Ethic* (New York: Macmillan, 1966). Because he employs a phenomenological point of view, Winter does not incorporate an ontic interpretation in the constructive portions of his analysis.

3. The classic formulation of Weber's point of view is found in the last part of his famous essay, "Science as a Vocation," in Hans Gerth and C. Wright Mills, editors, *From Max Weber: Essays in Sociology.* The most extended development of H. Richard Niebuhr's version of the fact-value dichotomy is found in Chapters I to III of *The Meaning of Revelation.*

4. Emile Durkheim's views are most sharply formulated in *Sociology and Philosophy* and *The Elementary Forms of the Religious Life.* Max Weber's clearest formulations are found in the two essays "Politics as a Vocation" and "Science as a Vocation" in Hans Gerth and C. Wright Mills, editors, *From Max Weber: Essays in Sociology.* For a detailed discussion of these matters, see Chapter VI and VII.

5. Compare, for example, Kenneth Underwood's *Protestant and Catholic* (Boston: The Beacon Press, 1957) with Herve Carrier's *The Sociology of Religious Belonging* (New York: Herder and Herder, 1965). Because both of these authors affirm a transcendent referent, their relations to Weber and to Durkheim, respectively, are ambiguous.

6. Kenneth Underwood, *Protestant and Catholic;* Paul Harrison, *Authority and Power in the Free Church Tradition* (Princeton: Princeton University Press, 1959); and Henry Clark, *The Church and Residential Desegregation* (New Haven: College and University Press, 1965).

7. W. Lloyd Warner, *The Family of God.*

8. See especially, Sigmund Freud's *The Future of an Illusion* and *Moses and Monotheism.*

9. Charles Y. Glock, "The Role of Deprivation in the Origin and Evolution of Religious Groups," in Robert Lee and Martin Marty, editors, *Religion and Social Conflict* (New York: Oxford University Press, 1964).

10. In this connection, it is instructive to note the references in the sociological literature to the writings of H. Richard Niebuhr. His study, *The Social Sources of Denominationalism* (New York: Henry Holt and Co., 1929), which focused upon the external factors shaping religious institutions in the United States, is frequently cited by sociologists. His *The Kingdom of God in America* (New York: Harper & Brothers, 1937), which focused upon the inner meaning of the religious tradition in the United States, is less frequently noted by sociologists. Because Niebuhr affirms the fact-value distinction noted earlier, this differential appropriation is coherent with Niebuhr's own constructive understanding of the relation between scientific and confessional studies.

11. See, for example, Gordon Allport, *The Individual and His Religion* (New York: Macmillan, 1950); Kingsley Davis, *Human Society;* N. J. Demerath III, *Social Class in American Protestantism;* Erich Fromm, *Escape from Freedom* (New York: Farrar and Rinehart, 1941); Charles Y. Glock, "The Role of Deprivation in the Origin and Evolution of Religious Groups"; Charles Y. Glock and Rodney Stark, *Religion and Society in Tension* (Chicago: Rand McNally & Co., 1965); Thomas Hoult, *The Sociology of Religion;* Gerhard Lenski, *The Religious Factor;* Talcott Parsons, *The Social System;* Guy Swanson, *The Birth of the Gods* (Ann Arbor: University of Michigan Press, 1964); Glenn Vernon, *Sociology of Religion* (New York: McGraw-Hill Book Company, 1962); W. Lloyd Warner and associates, *Democracy in Jonesville;* W. Lloyd Warner, *The Family of God;* J. Milton Yinger, *Religion, Society and the Individual* and *Sociology Looks at Religion.*

12. See, for example, Henry N. Wieman, *The Source of Human Good* (Chicago: University of Chicago Press, 1946).

13. See, for example Swami Prabhavananda and Frederick Manchester, translators, *The Upanishads* (New York: The New American Library, 1951).

14. Illustrative references in this chapter are confined to theologians within the Christian tradition. The author's special concern with and knowledge of the theological writings in this tradition have contributed to this decision. Analogous formulations are, of course, discernible in other religious traditions, and interpretations representative of most of the options cited here may be found within them.

15. See, for example, Karl Barth, *The Word of God and the Word of Man* and *The Doctrine of the Word of God* (New York: Charles Scribner's Sons, 1936) and H. Richard Niebuhr, *The Meaning of Revelation.*

16. Harvey Cox, *The Secular City* (New York: Macmillan, 1965).

17. See, for example, Jacques Maritain, *The Degrees of Knowledge* (New York: Charles Scribner's Sons, 1959) and Johannes Messner, *Social Ethics: Natural Law in the Modern World* (St. Louis: B. Herder Book Company, 1965). There are, of course, significant internal disagreements among theologians who affirm the same fundamental perspective. See, for example, the writings of John Courtney Murray on natural law to contrast a more "liberal" interpretation with Messner's more "conservative" view. The differences turn on the emphases given to freedom of choice in relation to the "form" embedded in the context and to the "form" relevant for a given problem.

18. See, for example, Reinhold Niebuhr, *The Nature and Destiny of Man,*

especially Volume I, Chapter V and Volume II, Chapter IX, and Paul Tillich, *Systematic Theology*. Niebuhr posits both general and special revelation; Tillich contrasts philosophical views which raise ultimate questions and theological views which answer these questions. Niebuhr uses Biblical categories in his analyses, but Tillich uses philosophical categories. In this way, Niebuhr accentuates the particularity of the Christian faith, but Tillich accentuates its universality. The difference is a matter of emphasis rather than of absolute contrast, for both affirm the universal particularity of the Christian faith.

19. Rudolph Otto, *The Idea of the Holy* (London: Oxford University Press, 1923).

20. The major philosophic proponents of this perspective are Alfred N. Whitehead and Charles Hartshorne. See, for example, Whitehead's *Process and Reality* and Hartshorne's *Man's Vision of God*. Recently, some Christian theologians have explored some dimensions of this perspective. See, for example, Schubert Ogden, *Christ Without Myth* (New York: Harper and Brothers, 1961); Bernard Meland, *Faith and Culture* (New York: Oxford University Press, 1953); and John B. Cobb, Jr., *A Christian Natural Theology* (Philadelphia: The Westminster Press, 1965).

21. See Max Weber, "Science as a Vocation," in Hans Gerth and C. Wright Mills, editors, *From Max Weber: Essays in Sociology* and the discussion in Chapter VII in this volume.

22. See, for example, Emile Durkheim, *The Elementary Forms of the Religious Life* and the discussion in Chapter VI of this volume.

23. See W. Lloyd Warner and associates, *Democracy in Jonesville* and W. Lloyd Warner, *The Family of God*.

24. Gerhard Lenski, *The Religious Factor*.

25. Compare and contrast, for example, the discussion of the Christian Church in Gerhard Lenski's *The Religious Factor* with James Gustafson's *Treasure in Earthen Vessels*. Lenski, concerned primarily with the external history of the church, focuses on causality, temporal sequence, and component parts in relation to a whole. Gustafson, interested primarily in the inner history of the church, focuses on human decision, memory involving the past, and a whole in relation to component parts. As noted earlier, one's view of fact-value relations conditions one's interpretation of the relation of internal and external history and one's judgment about the appropriate method of studying human phenomena.

26. See, for example, Peter Berger, *The Noise of Solemn Assemblies* (Garden City: Doubleday and Company, 1961); Will Herberg, *Protestant, Catholic, Jew;* and Martin E. Marty, *The New Shape of American Religion* (New York: Harper and Brothers, 1959).

27. See, for example, the formulations by Nils Ehrenstrom in Nils Ehrenstrom and Walter G. Muelder, editors, *Institutionalism and Church Unity* (New York: Association Press, 1963).

28. See, for example, Harvey Cox, *The Secular City* and Richard Shaull, "Revolutionary Change in Theological Perspective" in John C. Bennett, editor, *Christian Social Ethics in a Changing World* (New York: Association Press, London: SCM Press, 1966).

29. See, for example, Jacques Maritain, *Moral Philosophy* (New York:

Charles Scribner's Sons, 1964). Maritain tries to combine universal principles with their peculiar and unique embodiment in a special religious institution.

30. Reinhold Niebuhr, *The Nature and Destiny of Man*, especially Volume I, Chapter V.

31. See Rudolph Otto, *The Idea of the Holy*.

32. See, for example, Alfred N. Whitehead, *Religion in the Making* (New York: Macmillan, 1926), *Process and Reality*, and *Adventures of Ideas*. See Chapter XII for a discussion of the principles of justice and forms of social organization which may serve to guide such judgments.

33. See the references in the preceding section for exemplars of the various perspectives discussed here.

34. See Chapter IV for an extended consideration of this issue.

35. W. Lloyd Warner, informed by a Durkheimian perspective, has placed great emphasis upon these phenomena. See, for example, his treatment of symbolic occasions in *Democracy in Jonesville* and *The Family of God*.

36. See Chapter XII for a discussion of the grounds for these judgments. These observations do not imply, of course, that any of these institutions are functioning in a wholly satisfactory fashion in contemporary American society; but they do imply a rejection of extreme criticism of existing social institutions in the United States. Empirical material is crucial for an evaluation of a given context and for an assessment of the extent to which a given society is reflecting these ideals.

37. For more negative interpretations, see Gibson Winter, *The Suburban Captivity of the Churches* (Garden City: Doubleday and Company, 1961) or Peter Berger, *The Noise of Solemn Assemblies*.

38. This problem is discussed in fuller detail in Chapter XII. For an evocative discussion of this church-culture-society issue in the framework of a classical theological perspective, see Paul Ramsey, *Who Speaks For The Church?* (Nashville and New York: Abingdon Press, 1967). Ramsey criticizes the detailed and specific pronouncements on social issues advanced by various ecclesiastical bodies.

39. Although the informing structures differ markedly from the one guiding this discussior, both H. Richard Niebuhr and James M. Gustafson advance ambiguously positive interpretations of existing and emerging church forms in the United States and of the relation of religion to culture. See, for example, H. Richard Niebuhr, *The Purpose of the Church and Its Ministry*, in collaboration with Daniel D. Williams and James M. Gustafson, and James M. Gustafson, *Treasure in Earthen Vessels*.

40. These desired inner qualities parallel the ones Max Weber suggested for a statesman or true politician. See Max Weber, "Politics as a Vocation" in Hans H. Gerth and C. Wright Mills, editors, *From Max Weber: Essays in Sociology*, pp. 114-128.

Notes to Chapter XII

1. See, for example, Paul Tillich, *Love, Power, and Justice.*

2. This formulation may be compared with the typology of H. Richard Niebuhr. In *Christ and Culture* (New York: Harper and Bros., 1951), he delineated three broad types of Christian ethics. Although Niebuhr's typology is apparently not exhaustive, the two typologies are closely related because both are grounded on the relations of independence, contiguity, overlap, and identity.

3. See, for example, Paul Lehmann, *Ethics in a Christian Context* (New York: Harper and Row, 1963). Joseph Fletcher manifests an even stronger contextual emphasis; see Joseph Fletcher, *Situation Ethics* (Philadelphia: Westminster Press, 1966).

4. Contrast, for example, T. S. Eliot's *The Idea of a Christian Society* (New York: Harcourt, Brace and Co., 1940) with Reinhold Niebuhr's *The Children of Light and the Children of Darkness* (New York: Charles Scribner's Sons, 1944).

5. See, for example, Reinhold Niebuhr, *The Children of Light and the Children of Darkness.*

6. See the discussion of Max Weber in Chapter VII and Talcott Parsons in Chapter VIII. The reader is also referred to essays by Philip Selznick, "Natural Law and Sociology," and by Harvey Wheeler, "Natural Law and Human Culture," in *Natural Law and Modern Society,* edited by John Cogley (Cleveland and New York: The World Publishing Company, 1963) for contemporary perspectives which reject a transcendent framework for love and justice.

7. This discussion confines the analysis to human experience. Although the question of whether there is loss from God's point of view is not considered systematically, it is held here that those proponents of dipolar theism who maintain that the world's contribution to the Divine life is retained perfectly and everlastingly by God are correct. The priority of His mental pole and His once-for-all envisagement of all potentiality mean that He is able to contrast supremely all that might be with all that is and to appropriate totally that which the world has to offer to Him.

8. For an excellent discussion of the problem of equality and excellence from a different perspective, see Daniel Jenkins, *Equality and Excellence* (London: SCM Press, 1962).

9. For perceptive analyses of various facets of these processes, see J. K. Galbraith, *The New Industrial State* (New York: Houghton, Mifflin Company, 1967); Jacques Ellul, *The Technological Society* (New York: Knopf, 1964); Marshall McLuhan, *Understanding Media: The Extensions of Man* (New York: McGraw-Hill Book Company, 1964); Lewis Mumford, *The Culture of Cities* (New York: Harcourt, Brace and Co., 1938); David Riesman, with Reuel Denney and Nathan Glazer, *The Lonely Crowd* (New Haven: Yale University Press, 1950); and Maurice Stein, *The Eclipse of Community.*

10. See Peter Berger, *The Noise of Solemn Assemblies* and Gibson Winter, *The Suburban Captivity of the Churches.*

11. See, for example, Harvey Cox, *The Secular City* and J. Archie Hargraves, *Stop Pussyfooting Through a Revolution* (New York: Stewardship Council, United Church of Christ, 1963).

Index